EXTREME LEADERSHIP

with Four Case Studies in Vision and Determination

by

Charles Patton

2022

TABLE OF CONTENTS

PREFACE

This book is more a homage to the work of others than the presentation of startling new discoveries by the author. In cases where the work of others has been cited, quoted or incorporated, the author has given appropriate attribution. Some of the incorporated historical content comes from antique books, which were published in the 1800's and are no longer in print. More recent findings have also been incorporated with proper deference to the originating experts. The author's contribution is in seeing the common threads within the experiences of extreme leaders and extracting from those observations the common skills utilized by extreme leaders in extreme circumstances.

I would like to thank the great historians who so diligently captured the lives and tribulations of the great leaders so that we would have this material to evaluate and consider (see References). I have used their words far beyond the normal random quotation and in fact have used predominantly their original words because I could hardly improve upon them and because their words reflect the language of the times and circumstances far better than I could render. In the case studies, I have presented their words and their ideas with only the occasional editing for readability or additional observation added by me. In the body of the book, aside from where citations are made to the credit of other authors, the content is the original work of the author.

I would also like to thank David Lady who inspired me to pull together information, collected over the years, to create this book and Geoffrey Wilson who assisted not only with editing but also improved the readability of this book.

INTRODUCTION

It has been said that extreme situations call for extreme measures. I would add that extreme situations require a unique set of leadership skills. This book explores leadership skills, particularly those used in extreme circumstances. This book will help those who want to learn to be leaders and also help those who are already in leadership positions learn how to lead better and especially how to manage in a crisis.

This book contains a collection of case studies that talk about extreme leaders and their actual experiences. We recommend you read all four case studies first, although it is not a perquisite for understanding the content that precedes them. After you have read all four, you will begin to see the patterns emerge that are discussed in the body of this book. Your purpose in reading this material is to search within yourself to see if you can find your purpose in life and a Big Vision that you can pursue with the characteristics described below. Begin with purpose.

In leading, a leader must know the purpose of leading. Joan of Arc was an extreme leader who knew her purpose. Joan of Arc's French name was Jehanned'Arc but she preferred to be called Jehanne la Pucelle (www. maidofheaven.com/joanofarc_jeannedarc_jehannedarc.asp). When Joan of Arc was asked about her wish to lead the war to drive the English from French soil and place the crown on the Dauphin (heir to the throne) Charles V, she answered, "It is not a wish; it is a purpose." Leaders have a vision and understand their purpose and the difference between a wish and an intended purpose.

Leadership in extreme situations, in crises, during extraordinary times or simply during ordinary times can be directed toward good or evil purposes. The morality of the leader's ethics must always be questioned by supporters as well as opponents. So, we must consider the morality of the leader's purposes when considering extreme leadership skills. Even in studying leadership that has evil purposes, we can learn which techniques worked and which didn't. Common characteristics can be found among the skills of those who lead in extreme circumstances, whether they lead with good or evil purposes.

As a first brief example of an extreme leader, consider the actions of Mayor Giuliani immediately after the attacks on Sep. 11, 2001. He was subsequently hailed as performing well under those horrendous circumstances and was cited as an example of an extreme leader who led effectively. Clearly, his purpose was for good and opposed to evil. What did Giuliani do that made him effective during those critical days?

On the other extreme, consider how Cortes led his followers to invade Mexico in an extreme expedition, supposedly to claim the country for his monarch and to convert its natives to his religion, but really for the more evil purpose of trading for or stealing gold for himself and his sponsors. The skills that leaders such as these used are what this book explores.

Extreme leadership is mostly a story about extreme leaders who were male, but only because world history had not yet provided women with many opportunities to lead in extreme situations. We do have examples of women who were extreme leaders but they are few. Joan of Arc is one good example. Mother Teresa is another. When women have placed themselves in extreme leadership situations they have demonstrated the same or better characteristics as their male counterparts, but virtually always with good purposes rather than evil. Golda Meir, Margaret Thatcher and Hillary Clinton were or are brave leaders and, although not all faced situations that might be considered as extreme as others, they all have demonstrated many of the characteristics of extreme leaders.

Consider this tale: A Knight Errant meets an evil wizard. The wizard throws all the magic he can summon at the knight, but the knight keeps coming. The knight has setbacks, is gravely injured, abandoned by most of his friends and runs out of all resources, but keeps coming. After experiencing hardship beyond imagination, deprivation of the worst kinds, and grievous injuries, the knight keeps coming on. At last, when no hope remains and conditions are at their worst, more tragedy strikes, and the knight must again rise from being struck down, rising beyond any level of commitment he ever imagined he could muster to carry on. After setback upon setback, trauma upon trauma, pain on top of pain, the knight keeps advancing. Even though he may or may not succeed in his quest, like Don Quixote, this knight is an example of an extreme leader; committed, determined, focused, unrelenting and indomitable. These are some of the traits of an extreme leader.

Leadership can be learned but when called upon to perform in an extreme situation it also requires a special sensitivity to the needs of those who might be followers, a unique form of courage and the willingness to accept the consequences of whatever will happen.

For example, if Eisenhower's plan to invade at Normandy had failed, and that was a genuine possibility, he would have destroyed his career but more importantly he would have placed the entire world in even greater jeopardy than it already was. How real was the possibility of his plan failing? Eisenhower carried in his pocket a paper on which he had written a short speech to be used in the event of failure, in which he would resign, accept the blame and apologize to the world. He was highly uncertain of success but he had the courage to make the decision to move forward anyway. We cannot even imagine his feelings at the moment he ordered the mission to start. Even the thought of failing, let alone the prospects of the consequences, must have been daunting.

This is the kind of courage that comes into play in extreme leadership — it falls somewhere on a scale ranging between "doing what must be done" and "Damn the torpedoes" – meaning risking everything on the outcome. It's not gambling, which is for personal gain, but it is the highest stakes possible against the riskiest odds.

CHAPTER I:

WHAT IS A LEADER UNDER NORMAL CIRCUMSTANCES?

Rather than beginning with definitions for words like leader, leadership and extreme leadership, start by considering the various characteristics that have been identified for leaders. Their characteristics will define the words.

When is a person a leader? A person cannot be considered a leader until after they have led. A person might have "leadership potential" but without trial by fire, that person cannot claim the title of leader. Similarly, a person can hold a leadership position and not yet truly be a leader because they have not been tested. An ordinary leader will have characteristics such as the following:

A leader steps forward willingly when opportunity arises or simply takes charge

Of course, being a leader starts by being put in a leadership role or creating that role. Oftentimes, being put into a leadership role is an honor bestowed by someone in power on someone who has demonstrated a presence about them, a personality, loyalty, a positive mental attitude or just a willingness to volunteer. Other times, a person simply steps forward and announces that they will take the lead.

— To truly become a leader, a person in a leadership position must make a difference — not "tries to make a difference" but actually does make a difference. Being in a leadership position doesn't make someone a leader; being considered a leader comes from what that person accomplishes while in the leadership position. Most leaders learn to become true leaders through experience, also known as trial and error (or trial and success).

Leaders who try but fail too many times might lose their following and their leadership position — and might no longer be viewed as leaders or as having leadership potential — and possibly be viewed as not ever having been a leader.

Leaders who try but fail may also learn important lessons from their failures. Following failures, some may quit and never lead again, some may find and move on to other leadership opportunities, and some may stay and fight through the issues.

Oftentimes, even those removed from a leadership position for failing will arise again in another leadership position and become an excellent leader because of lessons learned from those failures. Abraham Lincoln is a prime example (Fehrenbacher, 1992):

YEAR	FAILURES or SETBACKS	SUCCESSES
1832	Lost job Defeated for state legislature	Elected company captain of Illinois militia in Black Hawk War
1833	Failed in business	Appointed postmaster of New Salem, Illinois Appointed deputy surveyor of Sangamon County
1834		Elected to Illinois state legislature
1835	Sweetheart died	
1836	Had nervous breakdown	Re-elected to Illinois state legislature (running first in his district) Received license to practice law in Illinois state courts
1837		Led Whig delegation in moving Illinois state capital from Vandalia to Springfield Became law partner of John T. Stuart

YEAR	FAILURES or SETBACKS	SUCCESSES
1838	Defeated for Speaker	Nominated for Illinois House Speaker by Whig caucus Served as Whig floor leader Re-elected to Illinois House (running first in his district)
1839		Chosen presidential elector by first Whig convention
1840		Argues first case before Illinois Supreme Court Re-elected to Illinois state legislature
1841		Established new law practice with Stephen T. Logan
1842		Admitted to practice law in U.S. District Court
1843	Defeated for nomination for Congress	
1844		Established own law practice with William H. Herndon as junior partner
1846		Elected to Congress
1848	Lost renomination	Chose not to run for Congress, abiding by rule of rotation among Whigs
1849	Rejected for land officer	Admitted to practice law in U.S. Supreme Court Declined appointment as secretary and then as governor of Oregon
1854	Defeated for U.S. Senate	Elected to Illinois state legislature (but declined seat to run for U.S. Senate)
1856	Defeated for nomination for Vice President	
1858	Again defeated for U.S. Senate	
1860		Elected President

A leader leads even when not in a leadership role — being willing to take charge, willing to accept responsibility and capable of managing any role responsibly whenever the opportunity arises. Most leaders have an internal drive to be a leader — they want to be the one out front, taking the lead.

Others would rather follow, which is perfectly fine because only one can lead and not everyone is cut out for the stresses of leading. And, some would just as soon stay back and watch what others do. The old adage: Lead, Follow or get out of the way.

> Audy Murphy, a fifth grade drop-out from a poor family living in a small town in Texas, was rejected by the U.S. Army, Navy, and Marines for being too young, being too short, being under weight. After the Army finally accepted him as a private, he had to fight to be sent into combat. Once in combat, he became a World War II hero, the most decorated soldier, received the Medal of Honor and later became a successful movie star. He started out simply as a follower.

The only person who definitely will never lead is the one who stays home and avoids ever having the opportunity to become more than they are.

A leader has wisdom

Willingness to lead is often mistaken for leadership wisdom. An eager person who wants to become a leader will volunteer to lead whenever the opportunity arises and begin the process of gaining experience. And as such, a "new" leader will be energetic and display strong organizational skills, which will sometimes be misinterpreted as good leadership. What's missing is Leadership Wisdom. A solid leader has developed wisdom about the environment, people and subject-expertise needed to succeed in the endeavor. This wisdom typically arises from the depth of experience previously gained in "the fray." However, leadership wisdom does not come without leadership willingness but together wisdom and willingness are not enough to lead successfully without also knowing how to motivate followers.

A leader motivates

A leader motivates others to achieve an overall vision, usually represented by a series of goals. We call that their Big Vision which is the ultimate objective of their purpose. Motivation comes from the goals laid out by the leader – especially when the leader gains the concurrence of those who will follow. Creating positive motivation is something anyone can learn to do but not all can pull off. From my experience, the following are factors that affect motivation and build commitment:

1. Belief in the Goals: A team needs to believe in the worth of the goals. A team will sacrifice itself against overwhelming odds for a cause they believe in, no matter how difficult or risky, even if extreme action is needed to achieve them. A leader will go to great effort to ensure the importance of the goals is communicated to, understood by, and accepted by the followers.

2. Energy: Motivation requires energy from the leader – energy that stems from the enthusiasm of the leader. A lethargic environment will not inspire or motivate.

3. Commitment: If the leader doesn't display total commitment at all times to the mission, the followers will see it and conclude that their own commitment is not so important either. For example, a leader shouldn't ask people to work to 6:00 PM day after day and then go home every day at 4:30PM.

4. Inclusion: Team members need to feel they are insiders on the team, that they receive all information and all feedback, whether good or bad. Trust, loyalty and fair treatment are keys to sustaining inclusion and commitment. Communication must be thorough and timely.

5. Recognition: Individuals crave recognition, individually and as members of a team. The leader celebrates successes and rallies everyone around when failures are impending. Good leaders don't wait until the final objective is reached; they celebrate at every possible opportunity. The more a team celebrates extraordinary effort, the more likely team members are likely to put out similar extraordinary effort. Be cautioned, though, about singling people

11

out for recognition when others have sacrificed equally and are not being recognized. Here is a program that can avoid this problem:

> For many years, I have used a program called A.B.C.D. awards, which stands for "Above and Beyond the Call of Duty." In this awards program, any member of the team (including myself) can nominate anyone else on the team, anyone supporting the team and even themselves. Peer-to-peer and self-nominated awards help reduce the possibility of overlooking a contributor. The nomination application must describe what the person did that was truly above and beyond their normal job duties. As leader, if I concur with the nomination, and I never had a nomination I didn't agree with, then, before the team, I present to the award recipient a certificate describing why they were nominated, signed by the nominator and me, in a frame suitable for their workspace, and a check for $25 to $50 (depending on family size) with which to take their family out to dinner to celebrate their success. Some people collect a number of these certificates and set a great example to those who have not yet received an award.

6. <u>Rewards:</u> The team needs to believe that there will be a payoff at the end of the mission if they succeed, even if the reward is non-material, such as the opportunity for promotion, or simply a gratifying feeling for having done a good deed, such as eliminating a tyrant or voting an unethical politician out of power. Celebrating success at the end is critical to follower overall satisfaction.

Experience and the history of extreme leaders have shown that job security, good pay and comfortable working conditions are not essential for a high level of motivation. In fact, some of the greatest accomplishments have been achieved under the most uncomfortable conditions, such as when Neil Armstrong, Mike Collins and Buzz Aldrin flew to, circled and landed on the moon, or when Columbus sailed off to discover a new route to the Far East and found a new continent instead. People are willing to sacrifice tremendously for a cause they can believe in.

The strongest motivation is achieved when the extreme leaders give the authority and responsibility to their followers to develop the initiatives and plans needed to achieve the goals needed to achieve the Big Vision. The extreme leader, with possibly other senior leaders, may formulate the Big Vision and lay out a set of goals that must be achieved to reach the Big Vision. To achieve maximum buy-in, the leadership team will then turn these goals over to their followers. The leaders will offer supporting guidance and resources if and when requested and, only if necessary to keep the team focused, provide their own direction. By delegating to the followers the challenge of confirming the goals and working out the initiatives, schedules and deadlines needed to achieve the goals, the followers will readily assume the responsibility to carry out the initiatives because they helped make the plan and will give their all to accomplish their plan.

A leader is willing to takes risks

A leader has courage and is willing to take risks to make changes. Those in leadership roles who fail to take any risk sooner or later will be viewed as failed leaders. Leaders who take risks and win tend to be lionized and those who take risks and fail may still be recognized for making a valiant effort.

Also, leaders that spend too long assessing the risks often fail as well as do leaders who shoot from the hip and move forward without sufficiently assessing the risks. The successful leaders work in a range between having perfect information and not having enough.

General George S. Patton leaned toward one end of the range -- relying on less information and moving rapidly forward. Although, even he couldn't move his tanks faster than his fuel supplies could keep up. On the other hand, General Bernard Montgomery, at least in General Patton's view and even at times in General Eisenhower's view, moved far too slowly and took too long to assess risks and plan his missions. However, as the war turned out, both were successful generals, using two different styles, because they operated within the bounds of reasonable risk-taking.

A leader must know how to innovate

A leader needs to be innovative; especially when the team gets stuck or needs help to solve problems after being unable to come up with their own solutions or when timetables are threatened. This is where a leader's past experience and wisdom become essential for success.

A leader also knows how to elicit creativity from the team and from outsiders. A well-run brainstorming session almost always comes up with valuable improvements to any situation, even if done at the spur of the moment under fire. The leader knows when to start and when to end a brainstorming session, how to guide the discussion during the session, and how to refocus the team afterwards to incorporate the new ideas into the existing strategy. However, a leader always must be responsible for the decisions made, regardless of who originated the ideas.

A leader sets the example and sets the bar

A leader sets high expectations and goals for others but also makes independent contributions to the effort as well. A good leader doesn't just stand back and watch the plan become carried out. The efforts demonstrated by the leader demonstrate the level of the bar that the others are expected to jump over.

When Joan of Arc led her armies into battle, she rode out in front of them carrying a banner reflecting their mission – to rout the English from French soil. General Patton often could be found at the front checking on the condition of his men and their field commanders. Being at the front with the troops is what followers expect of a good leader.

Good leaders do not delegate all the difficult tasks but rather keep some of the hard challenges for themselves -- to show they are not above what they ask others to do. Good leaders are willing to do any task they delegate to their followers.

A good leader contributes to the team's efforts while maintaining the appropriate perspective on the overall effort. A good leader will step in at times and push and pull along with his team. A good leader never wants to send a signal to the team that the leader is better than anyone on the team. Teamwork is about a sense of equality. Egos have no place in a team-driven effort.

A leader provides rewards

In addition to the effect of rewards on motivation described earlier, a leader often gains the initial commitment by promises of "loot" – something of value to be gained at the end. Cortes offered his men a share of the gold he expected to find. The "loot" is not always material; it may be the satisfaction of doing something good for others. General Patton promised his men that they would win the war by "making the other dumb bastard die for his country." Rewards can be simply the mental satisfaction of successfully accomplishing the goals the team laid out for itself. A sense of accomplishment can be highly satisfying.

When I was young, during summer breaks from school, I worked at the Smith family dairy farm outside of the small town where I grew up in Illinois. Later in life, when I reflected back on those times I had a fond feeling for the experience because I recalled that the work was highly fulfilling. The work was physically very hard and tiring, working usually from 3:30AM to 10:00 PM six days a week. It was monetarily not very rewarding either, earning $40 per week. In thinking about why I recalled such hard work as being so fulfilling, I realized later in life that it was because at the end of every day, you could stand back and see what you accomplished that day – that stack of hay bales, that silo full of silage, the hundreds of gallons of milk harvested, the cows fed, etc. I found immediate feedback from seeing the results of my daily labor to be extraordinarily satisfying. It was what motivated me to rise to the challenge day after day and never tire of the work.

A good leader knows that seeing the results of one's efforts is motivating and will call out small successes as often as possible, as well as the large ones -- creating this feeling of fulfillment and a job well done.

A leader maintains a positive attitude and is visible

Leaders maintain a can-do attitude and are out front and visible to their followers and well as to superiors and associated third parties. The Power of Positive Thinking, as Norman Vincent Peale popularized starting in 1952 with his book of that title, still influences people today. (Peale, 1996)

"Formulate and stamp indelibly on your mind a mental picture of yourself as succeeding. Hold this picture tenaciously. Never permit it to fade. Your mind will seek to develop the picture...Do not build up obstacles in your imagination" (Peale, 1996)

Positive-minded people are effective people and those who succeed as leaders or as individual followers are positive thinkers.

Leaders have additional positive characteristics

In his book, *The Art of the Leader*, Dr. William A. Cohen, (Cohen, 1990, p. 79-86) identified the personal strengths of leaders. The strengths he identified, which will also apply to extreme leaders, include:

1. <u>Strength of mind</u> – self-control, self-confidence, courage under stress, and healthy instincts that come from experiences in the fray.

2. <u>Firmness</u> – stable views, based on consistent thought, which in turn comes from reflection, adoption of basic proven principles and the experience of proving those principles under fire. Firmness must be tempered with caring, fairness, dependability and trustworthiness.

3. <u>Sound Decision-Making</u> – The combined traits of thoroughness, quickness, and soundness of decision-making. A solid decision-maker in a time of crisis is worth thousands of advance studies, unnecessary risks, and corrected mistakes.

4. <u>Knowledge</u> – Knowledge of the opponent, current issues, and the characters, virtues, strengths and defects of those under the leader's command.

5. <u>Creativity</u> – Ability to come up with new solutions to old problems or an unthought-of solution to a new problem.

6. <u>Endurance</u> – The ability to withstand prolonged labors, which comes from being prepared.

7. <u>Staunchness</u> – The ability to recover from a single severe blow, which also comes from being prepared as well as being fit, mentally and physically.

In Dr. Cohen's list above, many of the traits are driven by the wisdom of experience. Items one through four, and seven, depend on prior experience. Item five might also benefit from the experience of what has worked or failed in the past.

Dr. Cohen also wrote that leaders need to be willing to take charge, accept risk, and accept and responsibly manage the power delegated to them. Leaders also need to know how to set high expectations and goals for others.

To his list, I would add that leaders with honorable purposes need honesty, integrity, trustworthiness, ethical behavior and honor. These additional traits are important in life and I believe essential for leaders under normal as well as extreme leadership circumstances. Leaders often have to make unpopular decisions, such as separation of ineffective or dissenting followers or going against the passions of the followers, based on the wisdom of their experiences. In these cases, if the leaders have the respect of their followers and are known to be honest, ethical, earnest, honorable, and transparently sincere, then their followers will accept tough decisions. Usually, when tough decisions are made, the followers already know in their hearts they are necessary. Without the respect of followers, making hard decisions can break down morale and destroy the followers' motivation.

Leaders learn how to "Win Friends and Influence People"

Norman Vincent Peale, in his ground-breaking book, *How to Win Friends and Influence People*, wrote that a leader's job often includes changing people's attitudes to affect their behavior. Some suggestions to accomplish behavior changes are: (Peale, 1996)

1. Begin with praise and honest appreciation.
2. Call attention to people's mistakes indirectly.
3. Talk about your own mistakes before criticizing another person.
4. Ask questions instead of giving direct orders.
5. Let the other person save face.
6. Praise the slightest improvement and praise every improvement.
7. Give the other person a fine reputation to live up to.
8. Use encouragement. Make faults seem easy to correct.
9. Make the other person happy about doing the thing you suggest.

The above characteristics are the basics of leadership. These are learned skills – you don't have to be born with them. A person aspiring to be a good leader should practice these skills while searching for the opportunity to step forward and take the lead.

If good leaders have the above characteristics, what characteristics do non-leaders have?

CHAPTER II:

NON-LEADER BEHAVIORS

Non-leaders come in a variety of types. Some might prefer to be a follower because they don't believe they have leadership ability. Some may already know they don't have leadership ability from self-evaluation or past experience. Some may fear the potential consequences of failure or just don't want the stress that comes with leading. There are many reasons for not wanting to be a leader. However, not being a leader and not being willing to be a devoted follower can be a problem for the team. Too often, some who don't want to be led or resist being led become critics of those who do lead. Some may be indifferent or complacent to the level of commitment surrounding them or even be downright malicious or actively undermine the effort. Often, they are jealous of the perquisites that come with leadership without being willing to make the corresponding sacrifices. Those who are indifferent, overly fearful, jealous or dangerous to the effort should be culled from the organization as soon as they are identified.

> <u>Warning:</u> Failure to quickly remove disruptive forces from an organization has often led to the failure of a project and the downfall of its leader.

Non-leaders/Non-followers avoid risks

A non-leader/non-follower will tend to demand job security and seek guaranteed pay so no risk is faced regardless of the success or failure of the endeavor. A non-leader/non-follower will be a strong advocate of seniority and generally opposed to pay for performance unless it will be over and above the already guaranteed pay and little energy will be required to qualify for it.

Non-leaders/Non-followers seek definition

A non-leader/non-follower expresses a strong need for clear "rules," defined expectations and stable job responsibilities. A non-leader/ non-follower talks about and puts an overemphasis on process, the chain of command, job descriptions, assigned responsibilities and policies, will be uncomfortable with ambiguity and fast change, and will resist change at every opportunity. A distinction needs to be made between non-leader/ non-followers who seek clear responsibility definition so they can limit their workload and subordinate leaders who seek clear responsibility so they know their leadership boundaries. The latter is good and necessary to optimize the assignment of responsibility while the former is meant to avoid responsibilities.

Non-leaders/Non-followers complain a lot

Non-leaders/non-followers will be critical of what others are doing, especially the endeavor as a whole. They won't have their own ideas for solving any of the problems complained about but that won't stop them from complaining. They suck the positivity and enthusiasm out of those around them.

Non-leaders/non-followers produce routine and repetitive output

Non-leaders/non-followers will tend to be plodders – doing the routine repetitive tasks that require little thinking and have little variation. They will resist taking on additional work or new tasks, claiming the current workload will not permit it, even though the workload is not all that taxing. Someone who comes in on time and leaves on time nearly every day and who shows little passion for the priority initiatives of the organization will typically be a non-leader/non-follower.

Non-Leaders/Non-followers lack clear and steady focus

Non-leaders/non-followers can be easily distracted, whether by marginal work assignments or cohorts who prefer to chat and gossip. They may need daily or frequent supervision to stay on point and to produce consistently or, if sufficiently entrenched, may be able to produce the same level of mediocre performance day after day. When asked to help in other areas, they will find reasons why they can't or complain that it is someone else's responsibility.

In some cases, such as in large organizations, non-leaders/non- followers could be viewed as being the grease that lubricates the wheels of an organization – and, in fact, they may be needed for large organizations to run smoothly but they are not the essential parts of the organization and would not survive in smaller entrepreneurial organizations. They cannot be allowed to affect the morale and performance of the key followers who are essential to the mission.

The important point about being able to recognize these characteristics among followers is that failure to recognize them can cause a leader to fail. Also, even good leaders may fail if they have some of these characteristics.

> **Warning:** Don't put people with these characteristics and behaviors into leadership or other critical positions.

Having non-leaders/non-followers in the organization is only one possible reason why a leader might fail.

CHAPTER III:

WHY LEADERS FAIL

Dr. Cohen also identified reasons why leaders fail. (Cohen, 1990, p. 246) A leader will fail who:

Can't get along

When leaders lack the ability to get along on one or more levels (up, down, or at the same level as peers), they tend to fail. Inability to get along can cut off critical inputs and resources as well as cut off access to important information. Inability to get along can also cause others to rise up and work against the primary mission or the leader.

Don't adapt to change

From my own experience, this is a major reason for leader failure. Being rigid, resisting change, sticking to the original plan (when the foundation of the plan has shifted), and not responding to critical changes in the surrounding environment can cause the downfall of a leader.

> Dr. Wang, from my personal experience, had at one time all of word processing in the control of his company, with a system called WPS. However, because he failed to adapt timely to the emergence of the PC, Windows and Microsoft Word, he lost the control he had achieved and in essence handed it over to Microsoft. (http://wang1200.org/history.html)

> Likewise, IBM lost the PC hardware battle to Dell when it couldn't match its costs and the operating system on PCs couldn't keep up with what Microsoft offered.
>
> Both companies at one point were in a position to totally dominate a market and both failed to adapt.

In fact, not adapting to change is on the opposite end of the spectrum from extreme leaders, as they are the ones who not only respond rapidly to change but who also drive change.

Times decisions wrong

Also, from my own experience, making a decision at the right time is critical. Being slow to respond when a decision is needed can be viewed as bad leadership. Alternatively, deciding too hastily can also be a leader's downfall. Sometimes taking time before making a decision is the right leadership decision and sometimes a decision must be made quickly, based solely on instincts. Obviously, the timing of making decisions is a critical skill of a good leader and typically comes only after considerable experience. Dr. Cohen identifies as part of this weakness: fear of action, inability to bring issues to a head, or to assess or accept the risk inherent in decisions.

Preoccupies himself with himself

When ego walks ahead of purpose, failure is assured. Leaders who are concerned solely about WIIFM (What's in it for me?) will lose followers because they will see or sense the self-interest.

Unable to rebound – inability to weather a setback

Too often, leaders get vested in their ideas, enamored by them and overconfident about them. When this happens, they are likely to miss signals that change is needed or that disaster is roaring down the track toward them like the Cannonball Express, that speeding passenger train that crashed into a stopped freight train in Dunlop, VA in June 1903. (http://crazycrashes. wordpress.com/2007/11/17/the-cannonball-express-head-on-with-another-train/)

Sometimes even in the face of overwhelming evidence that changing course has to be done, egocentric leaders will insist they know what's best and will keep plowing along on the old course in spite of the dangers others see. Such leaders are generally poor listeners because others who see the problems will be trying to tell them about the issues but the news will fall on deaf ears.

Fails to allow positive solutions to overcome the reasons for failure
There are natural balancing tendencies in organizations. When a problem or crisis arises, other members of the organization, outside sources, and superiors may be able to help -- if a leader is open to asking for and accepting help. Recognizing when help is needed and seeking it should never be viewed as a weakness in leadership style but rather a key strength. However, some higher level leaders harbor an attitude that they don't want to be bothered with problems that aren't delivered with a solution. This kind of leadership style is weak. A senior leader needs to be open and prepared to help direct-reports when they need help rather than jumping to the erroneous conclusion that they are failing and need to be replaced.

> Many entrepreneurs operate under the faulty idea that the best solution is to fire someone and replace them – too often the attitude is, as a friend Larry Darrah used to say, "The boss seems to think the smart guys all work somewhere else."

Also, sometimes situations solve themselves if you have patience and are willing to let the problem play itself out. If a leader is closed minded to these possibilities, failure is more likely and possibly assured.

Lacks deadlines, fails to monitor deadlines and/or fails to enforce adherence to them

Those without timelines are those without focus – the two go hand in hand. Beyond having deadlines, watching and enforcing them are essential leadership skills. The absence of deadlines, monitoring and enforcement are traits of a leader destined to fail. Leaders who can't control project scope creep or who allow deadlines to slip without thorough investigation and reassessment of the balance of the project timeline can count on more surprises.

Fails to correct errors as soon as they occur

Responding slowly or not at all when mistakes are made is sure to doom a leader. If the leader has made a mistake, the sooner it is acknowledged and corrected the better. If a subordinate made the mistake, an investigation is warranted to ensure the proper processes are in place to prevent such a mistake from happening again.

> My directions to my direct-reports have always included: "You can make a mistake and we will deal with it but don't make the same mistake twice and don't make too many different mistakes."

Fails to accept responsibility

The worst mistake leaders can make is to not take responsibility for the outcomes and consequences of their actions. If an endeavor fails, the last thing a leader should do is to claim to be a victim, blame others, blame his or her followers, or blame circumstances for what happened. A leader could almost always have done something different to prevent what happened. Even totally unexpected acts of God could have been mitigated if proper planning had been done.

Take the horrible consequences of the tsunami that hit Japan's nuclear power plants in 2011 as an example. The tsunami could not have been prevented but the protections built around the plants could have been higher and stronger and perhaps additional engineering could have provided for better back-up power options and other protections.

As the adage goes, "Hindsight is 20:20" but in every case where disaster happens (e.g. New Orleans levee breaches) the preparation planning could have been better, the engineering could have been more thorough, more money could have been spent, and the response could have been quicker. All of these "could haves" were some leader's responsibilities and they didn't - or were prevented from - doing the job they should have done.

Fails to muster what is needed to succeed

Whether what is needed to succeed is experience, resources, energy, enthusiasm, dedication, concentration and/or execution, failure to pull together what is needed to succeed will cause a leader to fail. In some cases, failure to act or taking the wrong action can cause someone to die. Life and death decisions are always the hardest to risk-assess and to make.

Imagine President Barack Obama sitting in the Situation Room and making the decision to send Seal Team Six into Pakistan to kill Osama Bin Laden. Our Special Forces teams are not invincible, although they may seem like it most of the time and are equal if not superior to the best fighting forces in the world, which makes the loss of any of them especially painful for their leaders. We have lost helicopters full of our soldiers in the Middle East too many times already. The risk in that decision, not just politically, but for Foreign Policy, was immense, yet he made it.

Courage and the best information possible are the elements essential to making a critical and dangerous decision.

There may be times when the current leader is failing, that a new leader will emerge and step into the leadership role -- by request of the superiors or the followers, or by their own volition. Failure creates opportunities for an emerging leader to take over the reins – but take care to not step up prematurely to depose a leader – before having the support of those who decide who is the leader. Otherwise, if the original leader recovers the support of those who originally put him or her in the leadership position, through persuasion and/or new successes, then the leader likely will be disposed to seek revenge, figuratively or literally.

Of course to be successful, leaders need followers and extreme leaders need highly committed followers.

CHAPTER IV:

WHO ARE THE FOLLOWERS?

If you consider the accomplishments of historic extreme leaders, not one of them could accomplish what they did alone. Edmund Hillary climbed Mt. Everest first but Tenzing Norgay, his Sherpa, was at his side. When Neil Armstrong stepped on the moon, he couldn't have done so without the help of Michael Collins piloting the Command Module, Buzz Aldrin landing the Lunar Module on the moon's surface and thousands of people at NASA who built their spaceships and guided them to the moon and back. And, if you consider Christopher Columbus, Hernando Cortes, Mahatma Gandhi and other extreme leaders throughout the years you might think that they accomplished what they did by stirring into a lather a large batch of bumbling, unthinking followers. But that thought would be wrong. Followers are not mindless. They often have very valuable skills and a high level of competence in applying those skills. They usually require little direction and are usually very loyal and as committed to accomplishing the vision as the leader. They may or may not have had the same vision as the leader nor the same ability to influence others but they can be just as committed to the mission and just as intrepid as the leader, fighting side-by-side in the midst of the fray. And, sometimes they may even sacrifice their lives to protect the leader.

Why do followers follow?

Regardless of whether a participant in the quest has the role of follower or intermediate leader, people do what they do for their own reasons, which are not necessarily the same as the extreme leader's reasons. Followers might volunteer with the hopes of gaining fame or fortune, or might do so with the hopes of advancing their career by carrying increased responsibility, or might do so out of friendship and/or love for the leader. Followers' reasons may differ from the extreme leader's reasons, which typically are founded upon a higher purpose, some spiritual inspiration, or a noble goal. And, for some followers, their reasons may be just as noble and/ or completely aligned with those of the leader.

However, regardless of their motives, followers must align their interests with those of the leader or at least identify with the interests of their leader; and in so doing align their future with that of the leader.

How are followers attracted?

Followers may be attracted just by the act of the leader stepping forward to address an issue about which they, too, have been concerned. Followers also may be attracted by the leader simply because the leader asked for help. Or, followers may come forth when word about the vision is communicated because they, too, believe in it or in some way sympathize with the leader.

The initial followers may attract more followers – by helping to spread the word. Followers may be attracted by the leader setting a public example of helping those who need help. For example, Martin Luther King's peaceful demonstrations brought more people to his cause.

Followers are most likely to be naturally drawn to a leader when the leader has recognized and begins to address a genuinely serious problem or opportunity.

How should followers be managed?

Followers should be managed like any work team. They should be given clear assignments, be kept well-informed, and be recognized when they accomplish their assignments.

Robert Townsend, author of *Up the Organization* and CEO of Avis Car Rental during the 1960s, said, "True leadership must be for the benefit of the followers, not the enrichment of the leaders." (http://thinkexist.com/quotes/with/keyword/followers/)

Followers can be organized into teams and positively energized through competition with other teams. Individual followers should be praised in public, disciplined in private.

During extreme circumstances, harsh and even cruel behavior by the leader may become necessary to maintain discipline and/or to enforce essential policies (e.g., Cortes ordered that women were not to be raped). Such harsh actions by a leader are likely to be judged later as having been necessary and acceptable, provided the endeavor was successful. If the endeavor was not successful, such harsh actions may be judged as being unnecessary and unduly harsh. If a harsh leader is successful, the behavior is likely to be forgiven. If a harsh leader is unsuccessful, the behavior may be pointed to as one of the reasons for failure, may in fact have been one of the causes of failure, and could even lead to prosecution for unlawful acts.

How are followers motivated?

Rewards have already been discussed -- delivered at the end of the mission and whenever an opportunity arises that can be celebrated along the way. Information sharing is another important motivator. People want to feel that they are insiders and an important part of the solution. If they are not kept informed, they will feel expendable. Treating them as special, such as actively seeking their opinions, is highly motivating. Respecting their opinions is even better.

Years ago, I helped lead several "Town Hall Meetings" in a company that was having morale issues. The purpose of the meetings was to air the issues. The ground rules were that decisions that could be made without further study would be made at the meeting. Decisions that needed research before being made would be deferred but a list would be posted with dates as to when the decision would be made and announced. The attendees would be told immediately when something requested could not be done at all because it didn't fit the company's strategies or policies. As a result of the meetings, a number of burning issues were settled and the attendees left understanding more about why some decisions could not be made, and that the remaining deferred decisions were being seriously considered. The meetings and the follow-up were very successful at resolving the attendees' frustrations and went a long way toward improving morale.

Resolving followers' issues promptly, openly and honestly is an excellent way to build trust and improve morale.

How are followers handled when discipline is needed?
The rules must be laid out clearly and violations of rules must be addressed swiftly, fairly and consistently. Sanctions must be applied when necessary. Encouragement must be given when needed. Recognition and rewards are important, as previously discussed, to balance the toughness that is needed from time to time.

Years ago, my managers labeled a discipline technique I used the "The Sandwich" because I always privately presented criticism of an employee's performance sandwiched between a.) Reminding them that they were valuable and had done many good deeds and c.) Letting them know that I had confidence that they would not repeat the same mistake again and would continue to do good work. In the middle: b.) was the criticism of what they weren't doing right with direction on what they should be doing.

Discipline is almost always necessary from time to time but, hopefully, the undesirable behavior that requires it will not be repeated.

Other follower treatment

Followers should be treated as if they are generals in their own right. If they feel responsible and are recognized for being responsible, they will act responsibly. Some will rise to the challenge and operate independently very successfully while others may not. The extreme leaders need to know their followers and their skills and capacities and that knowledge can best be gained by testing them with responsibility.

Not all will respond as generals; some will need orders that are simple and explicit and some may totally lack independence of mind. Most will have an innate willingness to obey orders and a wish to please, and all will respond to praise, rewards and recognition.

These are the traits of followers. The previously described traits of a leader are found in Extreme Leaders but to a greater degree, and with some additional characteristics.

CHAPTER V:

CHARACTERISTICS OF AN EXTREME LEADER

We've described the qualities of leaders, followers and non-leaders/ non-followers above. In considering the characteristics of the extreme leaders we've studied, we find they have all the characteristics of an ordinary leader but with a more intense level of commitment, focus and drive. They operate on a plane above ordinary leaders. Their distinguishing additional characteristics include:

They stand alone initially in believing in their Big Vision
Extreme leaders tend to be "out there alone" with no one else at first understanding or buying into their vision. Others will begin to feel the vision, relate to it, and be drawn to it but they won't understand it initially. Others will dispute it or even work against it, criticizing and discrediting the person bringing it forth as a dreamer, as Christopher Columbus was described, or as a charlatan or witch as Joan of Arc was described. Extreme leaders use their personal initiative to start a whole chain of events moving.

They tap into dissatisfaction with the status quo
Often, extreme leaders can sense great tension affecting the people around them that the people have been unwilling or afraid to acknowledge, speak about, or deal with. Joan of Arc tapped into the frustration of the French citizens who feared and hated the English invaders and wanted them gone

from France but were afraid to do anything about their condition until she stepped forward. Adolf Hitler came to power so easily because he promised the German people what they longed for – reinstatement of their pride and return of their economy back to what it was before the First World War. Peoples' dissatisfaction, like lightning, is a powerful force if a leader can capture and channel it.

They find courage

Extreme leaders find a way to summon the courage to face what others want faced but have been unwilling to face on their own. Many people will give their support to a leader as soon as the leader steps forward because they know their frustrations will continue unless they do.

They don't wait for someone else to step up

Extreme leaders find the courage to step forward and volunteer to lead people toward solving their most frustrating problems without waiting for someone to ask or tell them to. They don't wait for someone else to do it; they do it. Often, extreme leaders admit to having had great fear about what they would face, but they always found a higher purpose that drove them to face the challenge in spite of the dangers.

They attract followers

Extreme leaders are not afraid to be responsible for the mental and physical well-being of others. When the vision is right and the angst sufficiently painful, people will step up to be followers. In time they will become loyal and as brave as their leader.

Will risk all they own

Just like America's Founding Fathers put their fame, fortunes and lives on the line against the British, this is what extreme leaders do. Christopher Columbus, Hernando Cortes, Joan of Arc, and many others have rolled the dice, putting all their money, reputations and lives in the pot. Nothing sharpens the focus and energizes like having everything on the line. In some ways, putting it all out there is one of the extreme leader's sources of power and energy.

Their dreams are deemed implausible

The visions of extreme leaders are usually grand, seemingly impossible, and beyond most peoples' imaginations. Grand dreams are another source of their power because the grandness intrigues, fires the imagination and inspires. Often, they face insurmountable odds but somehow manage to surmount them anyway.

Their means are greater

They often begin with little in physical resources, money or supporters, relying on their personality to raise the resources they need. They raise resources because they possess charisma, a knack for persuasion, earnestness and, as Mark Twain called it "a transparency of sincerity." (Twain, 1899)

Extreme leaders often do not hold a position of leadership when the Vision comes to them. The leadership position comes about from their passion, commitment and persistence. Often, extreme leaders will have extraordinary willpower and patience as well.

> Christopher Columbus pursued the support of Queen Isabella for twelve years. Joan of Arc had to present her request and plead her case to the governor of Vaucouleurs for men-at-arms to escort her to go see the king three times over a year-long period.

They are moved more than others by the circumstances that try everyone's soul

Extreme leaders recognize the crisis going on around them and know deep down that it must be dealt with. This internal force helps leaders keep their head in an emergency, stand their ground when others are fleeing, and have the confidence in their abilities to survive no matter what is happening.

They are prepared to give their life to achieve their vision
Martin Luther King is one of the finest examples of an extreme leader. He saw wrongs that needed to be righted, wrongs that others saw but were doing little about. He created his vision for equality and then pursued it with an unrelenting passion – and ultimately gave his life for it.

> Extreme Leaders often anticipate that they will give their life for their cause. Martin Luther King knew. Joan of Arc knew. Mahatma Gandhi knew.

Not all extreme leaders die as a result of their quest (e.g., Giuliani, Patton and Cortes). Death is not a perquisite to extreme leaders achieving their Big Visions, but it can be a consequence.

They maintain a positive frame of mind regardless of setbacks
When faced with unexpected challenges, extreme leaders will rearrange priorities, set new priorities, and start new actions to keep progress moving toward the goals. They see opportunities others don't see. They find creative solutions when problems arise that appear insurmountable.

They face danger with a unique confidence
In some cases, extreme leaders may face extreme danger, may be trapped, and may have to fight nature's elements or a foe to escape. Sometimes, they are imprisoned and/or killed, as was the case for Joan of Arc, Martin Luther King, Nelson Mandela and others. However, they face such trials with grace and at times a resignation of the inevitable – inevitability that they had anticipated and contemplated.

They break unjust rules

In many cases, extreme leaders find they must violate the law or break societal or political rules because the rules are unjust or are preventing the accomplishment of their visions. Extreme leaders may break the rules peaceably (as Martin Luther King and Mahatma Gandhi did) but at other times they may need to resort to violence or force as did Nelson Mandela before he was imprisoned and, as you will read in his case study, Cortes when he snuck his ships out of the harbor. Violence is a measure of last resort for extreme leaders with good purposes. Those with evil purposes employ violence as a tool for grabbing power and perpetrating their evil deeds.

They draw their authority from a higher authority

In some cases, extreme leaders may believe that a higher calling is behind their actions – from religious fervor or simply pure enlightenment. Extreme leaders are driven by a force that comes from deep inside them and may at times be supported from outside by spiritual enlightenment or guidance.

They leave a lasting impact

With a Big Vision, whether successful or not, extreme leaders will have made a lasting impact regardless of outcome. Adolf Hitler killed millions of Jews – that is a lasting impact of the worst kind. Joan of Arc freed France from the English – that had a lasting impact of the best kind. The flight to walk on the moon – that too made its everlasting mark.

They are clear-headed and mentally strong

Extreme leaders may be hard or soft physically but will know what they want and what has to be done to get it. They will be mentally sharp and crystal clear in convincing others to their vision and viewpoint.

They know how to function in an insecure environment driven by high expectations

Extreme leaders may only be as secure as their last victory. Napoleon won and then lost major battles, was exiled, came back to lead more major battles and then lost a big one with Russia. Then, he was exiled by his supporters.

For extreme leaders, the standards are set high – one defeat may be tolerated but when more defeats arise, confidence can quickly wane and supporters may start to drift away or turn on the leaders, which compounds the leaders' problems, making matters worse – putting the situation into a death spiral.

They tend to be sensitive to those around them

Extreme leaders build, discover, conquer, invent, create, and/or achieve new vistas … but they also soothe, listen, heal, touch, or bless, as Mother Teresa did always and Joan of Arc did often. Even Cortes had his moments (e.g., he once forgave a mutineer who was a likeable man; although he did hang him later for a second offence.)

> "Humility must always be the portion of any man who receives acclaim earned in the blood of his followers and the sacrifices of his friends," Dwight D. Eisenhower (www.brainyquote.com/quotes/keywords/followers.html)

Extreme leaders maintain humility at all times.

They obtain help from those more powerful or wealthy

Most if not all extreme leaders have been helped along the way by people more powerful and wealthy but they also didn't let that support influence or divert them from their ideals. A leader who makes decisions primarily based on personal gain does not qualify in our definition of an extreme leader – there is no nobility in their purpose.

Dr. Cohen also spelled out seven steps for leaders taking charge in the midst of a situation, which approaches the concept of extreme circumstances. He believes a leader in the midst of a situation will:

1. <u>Establish the objective</u> – making clear the reasons why the effort is necessary and important.

2. <u>Communicate</u> -- calmly, loudly, clearly, even colorfully.

3. <u>Act boldly but not recklessly</u> – not wait for more information or risk the possibilities of delay, changing circumstances, lost opportunities, competitors getting there before them, or followers losing heart.

4. <u>Decide and communicate decisions immediately</u> – once decisions are made it is important that everyone who needs to know is informed.

5. <u>Dominate the situation</u> – take positive actions to gain and maintain control and stay ahead of opponents and events. Also, they don't limit their expectations of what followers can do by accepting the followers' self-imposed or self-perceived limitations of what they think they can do.

6. <u>Lead by example</u> – be willing to do whatever followers are asked to do and take care of followers before they have to take care of themselves.

7. <u>Hire strong and fire weak</u> – replace those who perform poorly and cannot be redeemed, reprimand those in private who are likely to respond to positive feedback, and praise in public those who have performed well.

The above characteristics can be found in some measure among good leaders who rise to the challenge when confronted with extreme circumstances but these characteristics are found in greater measure among those who start out as extreme leaders. Extreme leaders have other qualities as well.

CHAPTER VI:

ADDITIONAL QUALITIES OF AN EXTREME LEADER

Extreme leaders are extraordinary – not as people but as visionaries and by their focus and commitment. In addition to the qualities previously described they may also have:

A Big Vision

Extreme leaders have a vision big enough to convince others to seek it with them. The vision, as mentioned earlier, is usually one that others will automatically respond to because they have harbored the same frustrations and/or beliefs. The Big Vision of extreme leaders usually entails great risk and yet is strong enough to attract followers who are willing to join in taking the extreme risks. Followers of extreme leaders are often very dedicated to the cause and willing to accept the risk for little if any ultimate reward beyond the success of the mission. Followers are rarely paid in proportion to their sacrifices and efforts, especially given the risks.

Perfect timing

Extreme leaders know when the time has come to act. Victor Hugo, the French poet, playwright, novelist and essayist said, "Nothing is more powerful that an idea whose time has come." He was talking about extreme leaders because they know before anyone else when the time has come. The timing is driven by the sentiments of the followers – when they have "had enough" to stand up and fight, that is the time for the extreme leader to step forth. One assessment the extreme leader is able to make is to judge when the will of the followers to fight exceeds the will of the opponents to resist.

Clarity of purpose

Extreme leaders have clearly defined in their minds the purpose of the mission – why they are making and asking others to make the sacrifices necessary to achieve the mission. There is no confusion and no cloudiness. Extreme leaders feel they are driven by predetermined destiny – they not only feel the destiny, they reach out and grab the role because they know it is their destiny to do so. The purpose of "good" extreme leaders is always a noble cause, constructive, and for the good of many. The purpose of "evil" extreme leaders may be selfishly motivated (e.g., quest for power), for the good of one or a few, or possibly even driven by a cause the evil leader considers noble but which society will eventually recognize as misguided and wrong, such as Hitler's goal to "purify the race."

Constancy of purpose

Clarity of purpose also demands, for an extreme leader, constancy of purpose. They must be undaunted by the risks they face. Disappointment does nothing more than delay the inevitable in the eyes of extreme leaders. Extreme leaders are not stopped by disappointment. They are not wearied by impediments or delays. Most times, they are not turned by overwhelming opposing forces. When driven away from their goal, they will double back and continue pursuit.

Passion

Extreme leaders have passion for their purpose that translates readily into passion for their Big Vision. The extreme leader's passion is what gets the followers' passions heated. For example Cortes' passion was for gold, which he combined with a passion for forming a religious crusade to conquer Mexico and convert the pagans.

Determination

Extreme leaders are not stopped by disappointment, impediments, uncontrollable delays, or even overwhelming opposing forces. Even when driven off course or away from the goal, extreme leaders will fight back, finding creative alternative solutions and persevering until their goal is achieved. Extreme leaders are willing to risk life, fortune, and even the success of the enterprise to achieve their core purpose. Extreme leaders will just as readily lay down their lives for their followers, knowing that to do so will inspire them to complete the mission. Extreme leaders are driven more by creed that conduct. Extreme leaders almost always start out as naïve idealists and end up as experienced and victorious generals or as respected and long remembered martyrs.

Preparation

Through experience, meditation, practice, reading, advisors (to a point), reading and training, many extreme leaders will have prepared themselves for their quest. When extreme leaders don't have resources available, they will create them as if from thin air by finding sympathetic supporters or gathering them along the way. Extreme leaders will often achieve vast accomplishments with seemingly inadequate means.

A caring nature

Extreme leaders are generally sensitive people, caring about each and every follower as well as others encountered along the way. They also can be magnanimous with the enemy as long as being so doesn't jeopardize the mission. Extreme leaders define the idea of a romantic enterprise without being romantic about it.

A take charge demeanor

Extreme leaders are not shy about taking charge. They often will step forward before others are ready for them to step forward, whether it is sponsors, followers or opponents. Extreme leaders quickly become the heart and soul of the endeavor. Extreme leaders know from the first moment the goal and general approach to achieving their purpose even if they don't know exactly how it will actually happen. Extreme leaders will be fully involved – in the thick of the fight, when fighting begins – leading the fighters and taking whatever comes at them. They will conduct all negotiations, intrigues and correspondence related to the matter. They will also often keep a diary or write commentaries as the mission progresses. Often, they have a full appreciation of the mark they are making on history. Extreme leaders will be cautious and calculating in their plans but will not delay unnecessarily. They are known to stroll among the followers during down times to pick up a sense of their condition and to look after their wellbeing, even standing with the person on hardest watch. During the pitch of battle, extreme leaders are so enlivened to see their plan being carried forward that their eyes have been described as glowing from deep inside.

Access to good generals

Extreme leaders attract good people, and often have a single close confidant as their chief of staff but along the way they attract others to serve as generals and help execute their plans.

Power over the minds of others

Extreme leaders know how to win the hearts of tough men and women and to attach themselves warmly to those who will be nearest to them. This trait is the genius of extreme leaders – the ability to bring together a miscellaneous collection of volunteers or highly underpaid followers and motivate them to fight under the leaders' standards for a cause that initially looks impossible.

Cortes, the early explorer (i.e. invader) of Mexico, is one example of an extreme leader. Among Cortes' entourage, some came for gold while others came for fame and yet others came to repair their reputations. Their qualifications were as reckless veterans, vagabonds fleeing justice, wild natives who had been sworn enemies of each other, and grasping hangers-on. They differed in race, language, social class, and interests – ingredients for in- fighting, jealousy, and factions. What Cortes did for them was to gather them into one place, convince them to work in harmony and one spirit toward a common meritorious principle and to grant him total authoritarian leadership over them.

Cortes did not dress to his station in life but rather dressed simply. He did maintain an air of dignity around himself, speaking with eloquence and locution, almost like a poet, but it was not an air of superiority. He was charitable to the poor and very patient with his men. He embarked on his venture with his men on an almost equal basis, allowing them to call him by his first name, Hernando. He would educate his captains in the study of the resources of the land, its social organization and its physical capabilities. He always kept his men in mind, putting them first before himself. The only exception to his informality was when it came to enforcing strict obedience and applying the severest of discipline. When angered he did not pale from enforcing obedience to the orders put in place for protecting their persons and property. However he would not reproach any man in public and would not stand for outrage being applied to opponents. He would never destroy without purpose. As a result, he often would turn staunch enemies into allies. He wished to leave a better culture behind, a higher civilization, according to the standards of the times. (Prescott, 1843)

Being an extreme leader also has its downsides. As happened to many historic extreme leaders, such as Mahatma Gandhi and Martin Luther King, their very success attracted enemies – whose ire was raised by the rapidity and grandeur of the extreme leader's successes, motives that were misunderstood, accusations of motives of personal aggrandizement, and imagined wrongs. Sometimes, extreme leaders have become disliked for their superiority of mind, developed through solid early education, voracious reading, writing elegance and gifts of talents for math, logistics, geography, and other skills of the times. Or, perhaps it was simple jealousy of their success as a human or a twisted desire to achieve immortality in the records of history.

CHAPTER VII:

EXTREME CHARACTERISTICS IN THE MIDST OF THE FRAY

Extreme leaders display characteristics and qualities among those described above during the formative process of organizing to go after their Big Vision. However, in the midst of the fray, other characteristics emerge. For example, it is one thing to be determined while convincing supporters to provide the needed resources and to talk key generals into joining your quest but to also display determination in the heat of battle takes determination to an entirely higher level.

Generally, when the battle begins, the extreme leader must be out front alone – leading the charge to encourage the followers to follow. For others to risk their lives and their livelihoods, the leader must be willing to do the same. Followers will be as intrepid and brave as their leader. Extreme leaders must be supremely confident in their ability to survive in extreme environments. Extreme leaders must stand their ground longer than the others and must keep their head in the crisis to survive.

Survival is the key to loyalty. Followers will commit their loyalty to leaders who lead successfully. If the leader is lost, then loyalty may begin to wane and extreme leaders know this but still risk their lives for the mission.

Extreme leaders must have superior ability when it comes to dealing with dissent. A rule that seems to apply to some extreme leaders in history has been to be the benevolent dictator – hang one and forgive the others, on the first offence. Most leaders will have their "metal tested" at some point in their term as leader. Followers and opponents need to know that a leader is willing to resort to the most extreme measures when provoked. Otherwise, like bullies in a school yard, provocations will simply escalate – taking advantage of the leader until the leader either reacts or retracts.

We learned (or you will learn) in the case study on Dr. Elisha Kane, captain of the Advance, the core plan to deal with dissent that can't be suppressed by force. When the ship became frozen in the ice and some of his men wanted to try to walk out 1,000 miles in the dead of winter, Dr. Kane faced a crisis. By maritime rules, Dr. Kane could not force the men to stay. So, he came up with this approach:

1. He laid out a new plan for those who would stay.
2. He gave the dissenters his blessing to leave and a more than fair share of the remaining stores.
3. He got those who would remain to buy into his plan.
4. He saw the dissenters off with the promise to take them back with a "brother's welcome" should they return.
5. As soon as the dissenters were gone, he immediately got those who remained to work on the new plan.

This is the basic plan for dealing with any extreme leadership situation.

Extreme leaders deal with setbacks

Extreme leaders face setbacks with resiliency and flexibility. When impacted by multiple setbacks, extreme leaders don't give up. Even when being beat-up, thrashed, and having to retreat, extreme leaders will find a way to recover and attack again. Extreme leaders are smart, though, too. Without giving up and foolishly wasting resources, extreme leaders may retreat, under the protection of a rear guard, to safer ground to regroup, reenergize and live to fight another day. Extreme leaders adapt to changing environments and circumstances and figure out creative ways to outsmart opponents and the elements. Extreme leaders will make unpopular decisions and then will think creatively, seeing options others don't. They will find options that will work and then inspire their followers to adjust to changing circumstances.

Extreme leaders have extreme resolve
Extreme leaders are resolute in driving toward the objective. They never give up, no matter the risk, dangers or obstacles. This resolve may be viewed by followers as super-human behavior but it really is simply super- human resolve. Extreme leaders will push the limits of human endurance and suffer extreme conditions as vast as their will. Also, extreme leaders will be able to see a way out of a crisis, even when it is deemed impossible by others.

Extreme leaders have an innate understanding of strategy
Extreme leaders develop an early interest in and an appreciation for strategy and through that interest develop an innate understanding of strategy. The elements of strategy are many but include principles such as maintaining a continuous balanced offense with rapid movement, improvisation, and elements of surprise. (Patton, 2009)

Extreme leaders are a keen judge of character and talent
Extreme leaders have an uncanny ability to pick the best followers. Extreme leaders do not pick just anyone who is willing to follow. They pick those who bring critical experience to the endeavor, who have the potential to be highly loyal, and who are already disposed to follow. While extreme leaders may look to those above for resources, the leaders' real power comes from below, from the people who follow, and these often require very little that money can buy.

Extreme leaders are knowledgeable of a wide range of relevant topics

Extreme leaders gain key knowledge about important relevant facts such as strategy, science and psychology through extensive reading, discussion and observation. They use their knowledge to target opponents' weaknesses such as when they are less decisive, slower, less willful, weaker, or disorganized.

In summary, extreme leaders are smart, knowledgeable, focused, committed, determined and more. Much of what an extreme leader is begins with deep reflection on the issues of the day and changes that are needed. Once the Big Vision is clear, the extreme leader then begins to attract followers and acquire other resources through wit and persuasion. Then the balance of the traits comes into play as the mission unfolds. Many of the traits needed for a leader to become an extreme leader can be learned.

CHAPTER VIII:

HOW TO DEVELOP EXTREME LEADER TRAITS

The preceding chapters describe the characteristics and qualities extreme leaders need to succeed. In this chapter we discuss how these traits are developed. An extreme leader has:

Strength of mind under duress

Training under the closest possible simulation of the expected environment is the best preparation for maintaining strength of mind in the fray. This is why police academy training includes live fire exercises in a mock village with pop-up targets that are randomly good or bad men or women. I went through this training once and one of the pop-up targets was a large woman holding a baby and pointing a gun at me. Finding the right decision is not always easy or clear when the problem presented is ambiguous.

Experience builds self-confidence as well as character, conditioning, and the ability to make quicker decisions. Courage in the face of fear cannot be promised simply by a leader doing simulated training exercises. However, the chances of a leader having his or her courage fail is increased if the leader has had little or no prior exposure to what might happen in the midst of the fray. A strong will can be developed also through meditation as well as training.

> Martial arts teachers tell the story that samurai were fearless in battle because they convinced themselves beforehand that they were already dead. By believing themselves dead, they had nothing more to fear. Whether this story is true or not, convincing yourself that you are already dead would take some strong spiritual conviction and if accomplished would allow one to act without fear.

Strength of mind requires self-control under duress and that comes primarily from experience or, if not from experience, then from an extremely strong conviction of purpose. One of the purposes of simulated training exercises and prior experience is to develop healthy instincts that can be called on later when the fray is real. A strong conviction of purpose may allow extreme leaders to drive right through a problem but an easier course of action might have been taken if the alternative action had been known from experience and avoided (e.g., through negotiation).

The strength of personal will, one that possesses the entire being of extreme leaders, is also their source of strength under duress. If they believe totally, with their whole being, in a cause, many obstacles can be plowed through and overcome.

An unshakable firmness

Extreme leaders have stable views, based on consistent thought, that stem from fundamental beliefs and principles, deep reflection, and experience "exercising" those principles. Principles need to be tested with followers to confirm they resonate and then tested under fire against opposition. Such firmness, in the eyes of extreme leaders, is often tempered with caring, fairness, dependability and trustworthiness. Also such firmness can be sensed by the opposition and in itself can be intimidating. Less committed foes shrink before fiercely committed attackers.

A combination of quickness and soundness of decision-making

Because extreme leaders think from a basis of solid beliefs and principles, they are able to make quicker decisions. Quick, sound decisions are worth thousands of advance studies, unnecessary risk-taking and time spent correcting mistakes. Quick decisions can be practiced in all aspects of life. Parents can begin teaching children to make decisions by giving children a choice and asking them to decide. Ask a child to make decisions often enough and under a variety of different circumstances and the child will grow up to be a decision-maker. Adults can learn to be decision-makers by increasing their tolerance for risk and making more decisions consciously quicker.

One of the keys to making a quick decision about any subject is to understand the consequences if the decision is wrong. The larger the consequences or the more uncertain a leader is about whether all of the possible consequences are known, the more time and care should be taken before making the decision. A quick decision over an insignificant matter has little risk and can be made with little if any supporting information. On the other hand, a decision needed in a hurry about an issue with wide- ranging ramifications should be postponed as long as practical to allow time to gather as much information as is reasonable in the available time. Making quick decisions is really all about making rapid risk assessments and this comes primarily from experience assessing risks.

Knowledge of their opponents

Extreme leaders learn all they can about their opponents – current, past and future. Extreme leaders are extremely well read, not just about opponents but about all subjects in general. They learn as much as possible from those who know or through building a spy network to gather information about the opponent's willpower, genius, decisiveness, and abilities to endure, be creative, and lead under fire. The key is to truly know who your opponent is. As George C. Scott called-out in his role as General George S. Patton in the movie, Patton, "Rommel, I read your book," as he looked over a monumental tank battle that the Americans were winning against the German Field Marshall Erwin "The Desert Fox" Rommel. By this he didn't mean he learned only his tank tactics but that he had learned how the enemy commander thought. Patton knew what Rommel would do in battle.

Knowledge of their followers

Extreme leaders learn and understand the issues that bother their followers, their followers' virtues and defects, and the degree to which they already share the leader's vision and purpose. Extreme leaders will know their frame of mind, frame of reference, ideals, biases, and personal characteristics such as honor, honesty, trustworthiness and ethics. The better the followers are known, the more clearly their purposes and mission can be aligned with those of their leaders. Developing an accurate judgment of people, resources and their capabilities, again, takes experience and strong will on the part of extreme leaders.

Creativity

One of the harder characteristics for someone aspiring to be an extreme leader to learn is creativity. Developing the ability to come up with a new solution to an old problem or an entirely new never-before-thought-of idea is not an easily learned skill but it can be learned through practice. The first step is to be prepared, like the Boy Scout motto. Being prepared means thinking about and anticipating what will be needed during the fray. This before-the-fact thinking, with "what if" scenarios worked out, provides a leader with a portfolio of prepared solutions and a framework for thinking of alternatives when the initial plan isn't working as expected.

Endurance

Extreme leaders have endurance as well, which is the ability to withstand prolonged labors. Endurance also comes from being prepared and being in condition – trained, fit, and mentally ready.

Principles and staunchness

The Boy Scout oath – to be trustworthy, loyal, friendly, courteous, kind, obedient, cheerful, thrifty, brave, clean and reverent, which I can still rattle off from my early days in the scouts, has a great deal of truth and value in it. These basic principles form the foundation of relationships with people and if you practice these from your youth, you will be a better person for it. There is a reason why young men who achieve the rank of Eagle Scout succeed in life and that is because they practiced these principles and trained in their youth to be leaders, goal-oriented and disciplined. And, extreme leaders have staunchness -- the ability to recover from a single, severe blow, either to themselves physically or to their plans. The ability to withstand set-backs again stems from being prepared, experienced and trained.

The ability to make unpopular decisions

Extreme leaders can eliminate or separate key resources when dissent occurs, performance is lacking, or disruptions distract the followers from their objective. Learning to make tough decisions follows easily, without learning, from the leaders' intense concentrations of effort toward the Big Vision because extreme leaders relate more to the Ends and less to the Means. Having a clear purpose provides a foundational basis for decision-making.

Bravery

Extreme leaders never waiver when others are counting on them. They fear being considered a coward as much as any follower. The followers trust their leaders and want to please them and don't want to be left behind, especially when the leaders have made them feel that staying is more dangerous than moving forward. So, bravery is what must be demonstrated and that comes from the mental mindset of the leader – action in spite of fear.

The right behavior

An extreme leader's behavior is more important than their followers' behaviors. Leaders must provide a balance of firm direction and personal enthusiasm for commonly supported goals.

Targeted communication skills

Extreme leaders' communications are oriented to promote unity of purpose, clear, focused, and full of word pictures, action verbs, and stated goals. Extreme leaders also listen to their followers – listen closely and keep them on point as well as make adjustments when their feedback warrants it. Extreme leaders' goal for communicating is information gathering, information sharing, support, team building, collaboration, providing direction, encouragement, allocating resources, recognition, and constructively reinforcing the rationale for decisions, the mission, and the Big Vision.

Can anyone learn to be an extreme leader? Probably not just anyone, but someone who really believes they can be one, is well on the way to being one. Can anyone learn to be a better leader? Of course they can. First, a leader must choose a good or evil purpose.

CHAPTER IX:

GOOD VERSUS EVIL EXTREME LEADERS

Extreme leaders with good, positive motives are to be supported and revered. Extreme leaders with evil, negative motives are to be promptly confronted and eliminated. Sometimes the perception of good or evil may depend on the observer's point of view. For example, there were Germans alive after Adolf Hitler's defeat in WW II, who still believed in his goals and purpose. There are still people alive today, such as the Neo-Nazis, who might think him admirable or a great man. However, based on the outcome of Adolf Hitler's actions, it is clear to nearly everyone on earth that what he did was evil, unconscionable, and from a perverted mindset. However, the evil leader never considers their objectives evil. They have formed in their own mind a justification – a rationale – that attaches a logical and in-their- mind noble purpose to their cause. This means that any extreme leader must consider very carefully and very thoroughly the validity of what they think is their noble cause. They must ask themselves: "How will their Big Vision be viewed in the light of history?"

If we judge extreme leaders historically based on the good or evil that came out of what they did, we usually can properly classify them. For example, Mahatma Gandhi is revered by many but there are probably still some Muslims who would disagree based on his being a Hindu, even though he supported all religions. Mother Teresa, a Catholic nun, would certainly be considered an extreme leader about whom few would disagree. Extreme leaders may be judged from their impact on history as well as by their mental state.

What was their mental state?

Some extreme leaders with evil purposes have lived under delusions of grandeur or paranoia or grand theories (Karl Marx, Adolph Hitler, and Hernando Cortes). However, extreme leaders can be judged by their results, their impact on all of society, and the classes and quantities of people helped.

How did they conduct themselves in the midst of the fray?

Extreme leaders can be judged by the example they set. Did they avoid risking their own lives but not hesitate to risk the lives of others? Did they stay behind when there was danger? Did they hold onto power beyond their prime?

How were they viewed by their followers in the end?

Extreme leaders can be judged by their followers. Were they lionized by their followers – afterwards as well as during the campaigns? Did their followers turn on them afterwards, based on the tide of public opinion? How did the extreme leaders respond to that lionization? Did they revel in the lionization or did they shy away from it with true humility?

Tests for identifying extreme leaders as evil

Extreme leaders can be judged by the morality of their purpose. Did the followers come to support their leader naturally or were they coerced by others or blindly following mob mentality? What level of self-esteem do the followers have? Are they low-esteem people? Are they easily swayed or confused? Did their leaders use propaganda? Are initiation processes and brainwashing methods used to create "cult-like" commitment? Did their leaders try to isolate them from the rest of the world? Did the leaders have an agenda not generally supported by more than a narrow group of followers who really didn't think for themselves and followed blindly based on their leaders' interpretations (or misinterpretations) of beliefs that mainstream holders of those beliefs didn't support? Are communications from their leaders limited only to those with a perceived need to know instead of being communicated openly for all to hear? Did the leader instill fear as a means to acquire and retain power? Was blind devotion to their leaders expected or demanded? Were followers treated in subservient ways and as disposable pawns or servants? Were ideas openly discussed or were some ideas forbidden as topics of discussion. Were the leaders trying to impose a radically new order, placing themselves in the position as the supreme leader and conqueror? Did the leaders resort to force without efforts to negotiate? Are the rights of those who were forced to change their behaviors respected in governing them going forward?

Groups with extreme leaders that fit the above descriptions include: radical terrorists attempting to further the Islamic religion through force and violence, such as those led by Osama Bin Laden before he was killed; Nazi Youth Camps run by Adolf Hitler before and during WW II, the Conquistadors led by Hernando Cortes, Jim Jones and his Peoples' Temple in Jonestown, Guiana, Napoleon and his French troops who attempted to conquer Russia, and Genghis Khan, who overran the largest land mass in history, to name a few of the evil ones. One main judgment that can be applied is: "What was the impact on the people in the area affected?" Are they all better or worse off?

Tests for identifying extreme leaders as good

On the other hand, good extreme leaders can be judged by how honorable their noble cause is. Is that cause one that rights a wrong rather than builds power? Does the leader serve his or her followers, rather than the other way around? Is the leader worried about his or her own rewards? Does society grow in acceptance of the leader's Big Vision as its accomplishment nears? Are communications pro-active, supportive and encouraging rather than filled with lies? Are the methods of governing such that others have a voice in governing? Is progress made through accelerating evolution rather than revolution? Does the leader die for the cause, as a consequence of accomplishing the Big Vision or during the aftermath of it? Does the fallen leader engender sympathy among the general society?

Examples of good leaders are Nelson Mandela, who completely reversed one of the most extremely radical and racially biased societies through his incredible perseverance, power of persuasion, and personal sacrifice. We have already mentioned Martin Luther King, Mahatma Gandhi, Mother Teresa, Dr. Elisha Kane, the first men on the moon: Aldrin, Armstrong and Collins, and Christopher Columbus. Others might include Winston Churchill, Dwight David Eisenhower, and Ernest Shackleton, the Antarctica explorer.

The judgment of whether extreme leaders' purposes were good or evil has changed over time and what extreme leadership means has changed over time.

CHAPTER X:

HOW EXTREME LEADERSHIP
HAS CHANGED OVER TIME

Over the centuries, the opportunity for Big Visions seems to have diminished as many were accomplished – from climbing the highest mountains to reaching the bottom of the Marianas Trench, from building railroads across America to building America's massive network of interstate highways, from flying around the earth to landing on the moon and from discovering unknown lands to discovering vast energy sources. It might seem that the Big Visions have all been achieved, but that is not the case. The world is still not at peace, world economies are still dominated by greedy self-serving manipulators, and we have vast unknowns across the universe to explore. We have not learned how to travel across light- years, explored all the depths of the oceans, or reached the center of earth. We have not discovered all the species of animals and plants. We have not yet learned how to preserve racial/cultural diversity while celebrating and respecting our differences. And, we still have massive religious differences and inter-religion power struggles. We will never complete all the Big Visions humans can envision.

In our early history, Big Visions were often about adventure, discovery, religious conversion, kingdom expansion, fame and scientific discovery. Today, Big Visions may still include discovery and adventure, but too often are about making money – oil exploration, patents, and new internet websites. However, the key leadership strategies are quite the same.

Some examples of key leadership strategies that still apply today are:

1. Timely action is a key to success in a crisis.
2. Implementation execution is a critical factor in successful actions.
3. Failure should never be reinforced.

Not only do the strategies remain the same, so do many of the consequences.

CHAPTER XI:

THE CONSEQUENCES
OF EXTREME LEADERSHIP

The societal consequences from the accomplishment or even the attempted accomplishment of extreme leaders' Big Visions are usually substantial – the ending of a war, the dominance of a group of people, the elimination of injustice, and more.

Leaders and especially extreme leaders work under great stress but rarely show it. They must have periodic doubts about whether or not they picked the right Big Vision and goals. Goals can be changed but if a vision was chosen that turns out to be impossible and others have sacrificed dearly in the attempt to achieve the vision, then leaders must worry about the consequences of their actions. Extreme leaders worry about getting sufficient resources and getting them in time. Extreme leaders must worry constantly about their followers. Are they getting the resources they need? Are they being cared for? Lastly, extreme leaders have to worry about how their followers are performing. Are they getting the job done? Are corrections needed? If a follower is not getting the job done, should they allow them more time or replace them with another performer. And, if someone is replaced, how long will it take them to get up to speed and be productive? How much risk is involved in making a change and what if that change doesn't make a difference? And, finally, what about the extreme leaders' fears for their own lives and safety – how much concern should be had? Leaders can't be cavalier about their own exposure to risk. These are just some of the worries of extreme leaders.

The consequences to extreme leaders are often the same regardless of success or failure. In the end, we all die but extreme leaders rarely die of natural causes. Extreme leaders may die at the moment of victory or very soon after, as General George S. Patton did. Or, extreme leaders may die at the moment the mission fails, as did Adolf Hitler. The death may be self-inflicted or even at the hands of the opponents as happened to Mahatma Gandhi and Martin Luther King or in retaliation from an opponent, like Osama Bin Laden. Or, death may come at the hands of previous supporters or even the hands of the person who was saved, as in the case of Joan of Arc.

If death doesn't come at the time of success or failure, extreme leaders often find it difficult to return to a calm life. Lawrence of Arabia, Hernando Cortes, and General George S. Patton, briefly, found civilian life tedious, frustrating and dull. They had achieved such highs and lows and lived such fast-paced lives that the slower pace of a peaceful life wore very hard on them. And, a few extreme leaders live long lives in continuous pursuit of their Big Vision, never completing it to their satisfaction, and die "in the saddle" so to speak, as did Mother Teresa.

Whether death comes by the hands of others or by one's own hands, it seems that few Extreme leaders live out their natural lives. Winston Churchill did; Dr. Elisha Kane did; Dwight D. Eisenhower did; and miraculously Neil Armstrong, Buzz Aldrin and Michael Collins still are.

If the extreme leaders' purposes were noble and good, those who survive may be lionized while still living but regardless will be remembered favorably in history. Those who had good purposes but die will be remembered as heroes, heroines, or saints. Those that survive but their purpose was evil will be remembered poorly in history and may even be convicted of their crimes and executed or jailed interminably, if they don't kill themselves first. Those who had evil purposes but die will be remembered as villains and for the evil deeds they did.

In conclusion

Are you an extreme leader or do you want to become one? If so, this is your roadmap. If not, that is fine too but you can emulate the skills and characteristics of the extreme leaders described above to make yourself into a very good leader or an excellent follower.

CASE STUDIES

CHRISTOPHER COLUMBUS

A Case Study of what a Big Vision and Persistence Can Achieve

Based on the Book
A History of the Life and Voyages of Christopher Columbus
By
Washington Irving

With excerpts, edits, paraphrasing and commentary
By
Charles Patton

Introduction

The following is excerpted and paraphrased from a marvelous account of Columbus by Washington Irving published in 1829 after Washington Irving reviewed the original ships' logs from Columbus' voyages to discover a new continent that would become North, Central and South America, and the Caribbean, where he first landed. (Irving, 1829)

His Vision

In the early 1470s, Christopher Columbus supported his family by making maps and charts. For a time he lived on what was then the newly discovered island of Porto Santo where he heard fabulous tales of islands lying to the west of the Canary Islands. These tales fired his imagination and led him to his Big Vision. Columbus formulated three basic ideas for his radical belief that the eastern regions of Asia could be found by sailing west. These are the bases for his core arguments:

1. The nature of things: By comparing Ptolemy's globe to an earlier map of Marinus of Tyre, he ascribed 24 hours of 15 degrees each for a total of 360 degrees to the equator. Recognizing that 15 hours had been known to the ancients extending from the Canary Islands to the city of Thinae in Asia (the eastern limits of the known world at that time), and the Portuguese had advanced the western frontier by discovering the Azores and Cape Verde Islands, equal to one hour more. By his estimates, 8 more hours or one-third of the world remained undiscovered.

2. The authority of learned writers: He cited the opinions of Aristotle, Seneca, and Pliny that one might pass from Cadiz to the Indies in a few days. He also cited Strabo who observed that the ocean surrounded the earth. He cited narratives of Marco Polo and John Mandeville, who traveled east in the 13th and 14th centuries, that spoke of Asia extending far to the east. From a copy of a letter from

Paulo Toscanelli, a Florence doctor, to Fernando Marinex, sent to Columbus in 1474, Paulo maintained that Columbus could arrive in India by a western course of 4,000 miles in a direct line from Lisbon to Mangi, near Cathay, the northern coast China.

3. The reports of respected navigators: Columbus listed evidence of land to the west suggested by items that had floated to the shores of the known world. For example, Martin Vincent, a pilot in the service of the king of Portugal, related that after sailing 450 leagues to the west of Cape St. Vincent, he had taken from the water, drifting from the west, a piece of carved wood which evidently had not been worked with an iron instrument. Pedro Correa, Columbus' brother-in-law, is likewise cited as having seen on the island of Porto Santo, a similar piece of wood, which had drifted from the same quarter. Columbus also had heard from the King of Portugal of some reeds of immense size that had floated to some of those islands, which Columbus thought he recognized from Ptolemy descriptions of reeds said to grow in India. Inhabitants of the Azores also reported trunks of large pine trees that did not grow there and the bodies of two men who washed up who had features different from those of any known race on earth.

From these three core arguments, Columbus concluded that undiscovered land lay in the western part of the ocean and was attainable, fertile and inhabited. The success of his undertaking depended on two errors of the most learned and profound philosophers – that Asia extended far to the east and the earth was smaller than commonly thought.

Once Columbus had his <u>Big Vision</u>, it influenced his entire character and conduct and he never spoke of it with any doubt or hesitancy. He also was moved by the opportunity to bring the true faith to Pagan lands.

> **How does this apply to Extreme Leadership skills?**
>
> Answer: To qualify as an extreme leader, a leader has to establish a bold vision – often one so big that only he or she believes in it. The extreme leader must be completely vested in and focused on accomplishing his or her Big Vision and will not be dissuaded by lack of resources, lack of support from others, or obstacles that appear insurmountable.

His First Attempt at Garnering Support

Years passed before Columbus pursued his idea because he was poor and believed he would need the approval of the King of Portugal, John II, who was engaged at the time in the exploration in Africa.

Even though the compass was in common use, mariners rarely ventured out of the sight of land. John II had, around this time, the early 1470s, called upon the most able astronomers and cosmographers of his kingdom to devise some means by which greater certainty might be given to navigation. They produced the astrolabe, forerunner of today's quadrant, allowing seamen to ascertain their distance from the equator by measuring the altitude of the sun. This freed ships from the coast and allowed them to retrace their course on the return trip.

King John II was concerned about finding a shorter route to India by going west and met with Columbus. Columbus described the immense riches of the island of Cipango, the first island he expected to reach. The King listened but was reluctant to back the new scheme because of the cost and trouble of his unaccomplished exploration of Africa. However, because Columbus' arguments were so solid he gave his consent. Columbus then demanded high and honorable titles and rewards worthy of his deeds and merits. The King considered Columbus to be vainglorious, fond of displaying his abilities, and given to fantastic fancies. The King referred the matter to Roderigo Joseph and his confessor Diego Ortiz de Cazadilla, Bishop of Ceuta. They treated the project as extravagant and VISIONARY, meant in this case as a bad word -- meaning irresponsible, impractical and nothing but dreams.

The King then referred the matter to his council, who generally condemned Columbus' proposal, as they were becoming hostile to all missions of discovery. The King was reminded that he was already engaged in war against the Moors of Barbary, as well as fighting pestilence, and that another venture would drain needed resources and divide the power of the nation. King John II listened to his counselors and their plan to keep Columbus in suspense while they dispatched a ship in the direction Columbus proposed, using maps they asked Columbus to submit for their review. The ship ran into storms and returned -- supporting the King's counselors in their ridicule of his project as extravagant and irrational. Columbus was indignant when he learned what they did and that they had used his maps, and as his wife had died, he departed secretly in 1484 from Lisbon, taking his son Diego with him to Genoa.

Columbus left Portugal owing money and was thereafter unable to return for that reason. After about a year, he presented his proposal to the republic of Genoa but they were not in favor of it due to the impact of war. They encouraged him to present his proposal to Venice, even though Venice had been at war with Genoa. In the meantime, Columbus sent his brother to present his proposal to King Henry VII in England, but he became distracted for a year or two by traveling off to discover the Cape of Good Hope.

Meanwhile, Columbus arrived in Spain with his son Diego, destitute, on his way to Huelra to seek his brother-in-law. He stopped at an ancient convent of Franciscan Friars dedicated to Santa Maria de Rabida to ask for a little bread and water for his son. The Prior, Friar Juan Perez de Marchena, observed their air and heard their accent and soon learned their particulars.

The Prior knew about geographical and nautical science from being close to Spain's eminent navigators in Palos and had traveled to the recently discovered islands and countries on the African coast. He was struck by Columbus' views. He invited Columbus and his son to stay at the priory and sent for Garcia Fernandez, the physician of Palos. He, too, became interested and veteran Palos navigators provided hints that corroborated Columbus' theory. One, Pedro de Velasco, persuaded that the proposed enterprise would be of utmost importance to his country, offered to give Columbus a favorable introduction to the court, being on intimate terms with Fernando de Talavera, prior of the monastery of Prado and confessor to the queen. He advised Columbus to present his proposal to the Spanish sovereigns. The prior gave Columbus a letter of recommendation to Talavera. The friar agreed to take charge of Columbus' son and educate him at the convent while he pursued his audience.

How does this apply to Extreme Leadership skills?

Answer: An extreme leader will need resources, and resources often can be obtained only by convincing others to believe in the Big Vision. This is accomplished by developing a convincing presentation and seeking out potential audiences who will listen to the case in favor of the Big Vision. The audiences don't necessarily need to have the resources needed but are sufficient supporters if they know others who have resources.

In Search of Support and Resources

In the spring of 1486, Columbus left the priory and set off with his letters of recommendation with fresh hopes. It was a brilliant time for the Spanish monarchy. Aragon and Castile united the Christian powers by the marriage of Ferdinand and Isabella. The whole force of Spain had been at war with the Moors for years and, at this time, the Spanish Army was in siege of the remaining Moor mountain stronghold around Granada.

While Ferdinand and Isabella were independent monarchs, their interests were aligned. Ferdinand was hardy, even majestic. His genius was clear and comprehensive, his judgment grave and certain, and he was devout in his religion and unrelenting in business. He was a great observer and judge of men and unparalleled in the science of politics. His policy was seen as cold, selfish and artful by some and as wise and prudent by others. He had three goals: 1.) Conquering the Moors, 2.) Expelling the Jews and 3.) Establishing the Inquisition in his dominions. He would do all three and be rewarded by Pope Innocent VIII, with the appellation of Most Catholic Majesty.

Isabella was well formed with great dignity and gracefulness and a combination of gravity and sweetness. She had blue eyes and auburn hair. She had a benign expression, firmness of purpose and earnestness of spirit. She exceeded Ferdinand in acuteness of genius, beauty, personal dignity and grandeur of soul. She mingled in his war counsels, engaged personally in his enterprises, and in some instances surpassed him in firmness and fearlessness, while being inspired with a truer idea of glory. Her focus was on reforming laws, healing the ills from protracted wars, and governing the people. She was greatly influenced by her religious advisers but remained hostile to every measure calculated to advance religion at the expense of humanity. She opposed the expulsion of the Jews and the establishment of the Inquisition but her confessors slowly vanquished her repugnance with them. She advocated clemency for the Moors while being the soul of war against Granada. She assembled the ablest men in literature and science as her counselors. She promoted art and knowledge.

Columbus arrived in Cordoba but was disappointed in his hopes of immediate sponsorship, finding it impossible to even get a hearing. Fernando de Talavera, prior of Prado, looked upon Columbus' plan as extravagant and impossible. As a stranger dressed in humble garb and offering magnificent speculations, he frankly did not believe Columbus. At the same time, the war on Granada was at its peak. The court was in the field, shifting from place to place. They had little time to consider foreign exploration.

Columbus stayed in Cordoba until fall, supporting himself by designing maps and charts. He slowly developed converts and friends. He remained enthusiastic and maintained his dignity. Alonzo de Quintanilla, comptroller of the finances of the Castile, became an effective advocate of Columbus' theory. Columbus also became acquainted with Antonio Geraldini, the Pope's nuncio, and his brother, Alexander Geraldini, preceptor to the younger children of the king and queen.

With the aid of these two friends, Columbus was introduced to the celebrated Pedro Gonzalez de Mendoza, archbishop of Toledo and grand cardinal of Spain, the most important person in court. He was always at the side of the King and Queen. He was respected for his clear understanding, eloquence, judiciousness, great quickness and capacity in business. He was an elegant scholar but little skilled in cosmology. When first presented with Columbus' theory, it struck Gonzalez as having some heretical ideas, incompatible with the form of the earth as described in the sacred scriptures. With further explanation, Columbus convinced Pedro that there could be nothing irreligious in attempting to expand the bounds of human knowledge and to ascertain the works of creation. Gonzalez saw the grandeur of the conception and bent to the force of Columbus' arguments and his noble and earnest manner.

The Grand Cardinal arranged an audience with the sovereigns. He appeared before them with modesty but possessed with a feeling that he was an instrument in the hand of heaven to accomplish its grand designs. Ferdinand perceived the scientific and practical foundation of Columbus' soaring imagination and magnificent speculations. He was excited but cool and wary, and determined to take the opinion of the most learned men in the kingdom and to be guided by their decision.

The King authorized Fernando de Talavera to assemble the most learned astronomers and cosmographers to hold a conference with Columbus, to consult together and then to make their report. During the course of his examination, Columbus was lodged and entertained with great hospitality at the Dominican convent of St. Stephen in Salamanca. The examiners were professors of astronomy, geography, mathematics, and other branches of science, together with various dignitaries of the church and learned friars. Columbus presented and defended his conclusions.

> **How does this apply to Extreme Leadership skills?**
>
> Answer: An Extreme Leader has solid confidence and conviction in the Big Vision and prepares well for the big opportunities. Often, a leader gets one "bite at the apple," meaning the right audience may only entertain the Big Vision once. Being prepared and being in the right place at the right time is the definition of being Lucky. Clearly, it is not luck but rather the result of sound planning and thorough preparation.

The Arguments Presented Against his Vision

The challenges Columbus had to contend with throughout the examination of his theory were powerful and were presented by powerful men.

The most powerful of the examiners were against him. Some saw Columbus as an adventurer and VISIONARY, a bad thing in their mind. Others were impatient. Columbus pleaded his case with his natural eloquence. When he began, only the friars of St. Stephan paid attention to him. The others appeared entrenched behind the dogged position that after thousands of years of "status quo," how could an ordinary man suggest that such a great discovery was possible? Columbus was the victim of Monastic bigotry and the imperfect state of science at that time. He was assailed with citations from the Bible and the testament, the book of Genesis, the psalms of David, the Prophets, the epistles and the gospels – as well as expositions of various saints, St. Chrysotome, St. Augustine, St. Jerome, St Gregory, St. Basil, and St. Ambrose, and Lactantious Firmianus.

They attacked Columbus's citation of Pliny who described the southern hemisphere as the exact opposite of the northern one – which they said would mean that those nations would not have been descended from Adam, that being impossible, and would discredit the Bible, which says all men are descended from one common parent. In the psalms, the heavens were said to be extended like a hide and that St. Paul compared the heavens to the covering of a tent, which they inferred was flat. Columbus was a devoutly religious man but in danger of being convicted not merely of error but of being a heretic.

Others more versed in science admitted to the globular form of earth and the possibility of an opposite and inhabitable hemisphere but held according to the ancients, that it would be impossible to arrive there due to the insupportable heat of the torrid zone, and even if the heat could be passed, the voyage would require at least three years because of the circumference of the earth. Those who would undertake it must perish from hunger and thirst, as it would be impossible to carry provisions for so long. Columbus was told on the authority of Epicurus that, admitting the earth to be spherical, it was inhabitable only in the northern hemisphere, and only that section was canopied by the heavens; and the opposite half was a chaos, a gulf, or a mere waste of water.

One of the more absurd objections advanced was that, should a ship even succeed in reaching, in this way, the extremity of India, she would never get back again, for the rotundity of the globe would present a kind of mountain that would be impossible to sail up and over with the most favorable wind.

> **How does this apply to Extreme Leadership skills?**
> Answer: An Extreme Leader will face strong resistance – naysayers disbelievers, and saboteurs. The leader must anticipate as much as possible and must not shrink in the face of bluster, innuendo, and attacks.

Columbus' Counterarguments

Columbus argued in response to the spiritual objections that the inspired writers were not speaking technically as cosmographers but figuratively in language addressed to all levels of comprehension. The commentaries of the fathers he treated with deference as pious homilies but not as philosophical propositions, which as philosophies would need to be either accepted or refuted. The objections drawn from ancient philosophers, he met boldly and ably upon equal terms, for he was deeply studied on all points of cosmography. He showed that the most illustrious of the sages believed both hemispheres to be inhabitable, though they imagined the Torrid Zone precluded travel, and he conclusively countered that objection, for he had voyaged to St. George la Mina, in Guinea, almost under the equatorial line and found that region not merely traversable, but abounding in population, in fruits and pasturage. He appeared as the plain and simple navigator somewhat daunted by the task and the august nature of his listeners. But he had a degree of religious feeling that gave him confidence. Others spoke of Columbus' commanding person, his elevated demeanor, and his air of authority, his bright eyes and persuasive intonations of his voice.

Diego de Deza, a worthy and learned St. Dominican friar and professor of theology at St. Stephan, saw wisdom in Columbus' unlearned talk and calmed the blind zeal of his more bigoted brethren. He obtained at least an unprejudiced hearing for Columbus.

The most difficult issue was to reconcile the plan of Columbus with the cosmography of Ptolemy, to which all scholars had implicit faith (earth at the center of the universe) – although Copernicus was at that moment devising a new model of the solar system with the sun at the center.

Conferences took place, prejudice remained, and the more liberal and intelligent felt little interest in the discussions, even those who listened regarded the plan as a delightful vision, full of promise but one that would never be realized.

Fernando de Talavera, to whom the matter was entrusted, had too little esteem for it and was too much occupied with the bustle of public concerns, to press it to a conclusion; and thus the inquiry experienced continual procrastination and neglect.

The consultations of the board at Salamanca were interrupted by the departure of the court to Cordova early in the spring of 1487, called away by war, the campaign against the wild, rugged and mountainous area around Malaga.

Fernando de Talavera, now bishop of Avila, traveled with the queen as her confessor. For a long time Columbus was kept in suspense.

Consideration of Columbus' proposals suffered from the ebbs and flows of the King's war. Whenever the court had an interval of leisure, they took up his affair, but then the hurry and tempest returned and the question was swept away again. In the meantime, Columbus was ridiculed as a dreamer, adventurer and madman. Children pointed to their heads as he walked by, meaning he was a crazy man.

However, Columbus had made an impression on several of the learned men – including his friend Friar Diego Deza, tutor to Prince Juan. In spite of the Junto of Salamanca, favor had grown in the court. Fernando de Talavera was commanded to inform Christopher Columbus, then at Cordova, that the great cares and expenses of the war rendered it impossible for them to engage in any new enterprises but when the war was concluded, they would have the time and inclination to consider what he offered.

Columbus was unwilling to receive the reply from someone who had always shown himself to be unfriendly. He repaired to the court of Seville to learn his fate from the monarchs' lips. Their reply was virtually the same – declining the enterprise in the present but holding out future hope. Columbus looked upon their answer as a mere evasive mode of getting rid of his importunity; he believed the Sovereigns prepossessed by the objections of the ignorant and the bigoted, and, giving up all hopes of help from the crown, he turned his back on Seville with disappointment and indignation.

Unwilling to break off his connection with Spain as he had found a tender tie with a lady from Cordova named Beatrix Enriquez, apparently of noble family, but not known to have been sanctioned with marriage. She was the mother of his second son, Fernando, who became his historian, and who Columbus treated on equal terms with his legitimate son, Diego.

> **How does this apply to Extreme Leadership skills?**
>
> Answer: An Extreme Leader must be prepared to handle all objections with solid counter-arguments. Prior practicing in front of trusted intelligent friends, who can simulate the most extreme attacks, is the best way to prepare. This is comparable to how a CEO prepares for a shareholder annual meeting – all the possible questions are thought up and answers pre-prepared for each.

Columbus Tries another Angle

Columbus, despairing of the court, turned to wealthy individuals, Spanish nobles. Among them were dukes of Medina Sidonia and Medina Celi. Both had estates like principalities, lying along the seashore, with ports and shipping. They served the monarchs more as princes than vassals, bringing armies of their retainers to the field, led by their own captains or themselves. They assisted with their armadas and contributed their treasures to the war. Sidonia sent a large force of cavaliers, 20,000 doblas of gold, and 100 vessels, some armed and others laden with provisions.

Columbus had many interviews and conversations, first with Medina Sidonia but came to no conclusions. The duke was initially tempted by the magnificent potential held out by Columbus but their very splendor implied exaggeration. He finally rejected the venture as the dream of an Italian visionary.

Columbus next turned to the Duke of Medina Celi and, for a time, with great prospect of success. At one point, the duke was on the verge of dispatching Columbus on the contemplated voyage with three or four caravels. After considering how the Crown would react (unfavorably), he suddenly abandoned his offer. The venture was too great an undertaking for a mere subject and fit only for a sovereign power. He did encourage Columbus to again apply to the monarchs and offered to use his influence with the queen.

Columbus in the meantime had received an encouraging letter from the King of France and lost no time in repairing to Paris. He went to La Rabida to seek his eldest son, Diego, still under the care of his zealous friend, Friar Juan Perez. After seven years' solicitation at the court, Columbus arrived on the doorstep of the friar, and the friar was greatly moved by the humility of his garb, his poverty and his disappointment. When the friar heard that the important enterprise was about to be lost to his country, he was moved.

His ardent spirit powerfully excited, he summoned and consulted with his friend and learned physician, Garcia Fernandez. He called in also the counsel of Martin Alonzo Pinzon, head of the wealthy and distinguished family of Navigators of Palos. Pinzon agreed to engage Columbus' plan with purse and person, offering to bear Columbus' expenses in a renewed application to the court. Friar Perez had been confessor to the queen and knew she was accessible.

Columbus was reluctant to leave Spain, which he felt was his home, but he was also reluctant to renew in another court the vexations and disappointments he experienced in Spain and Portugal. The little council cast about for an ambassador and chose Sebastian Rodriguez, a pilot of Lepi, one of the most shrewd and important people in this maritime neighborhood.

How does this apply to Extreme Leadership skills?

Answer: An Extreme Leader must be resilient and persistent. Becoming discouraged is easy; staying firm in resolve is one important trait that separates extreme leaders from leaders.

Columbus Tries Again

The queen was in Santa Fe, the military city built in the Vega before Grenada. Their ambassador, Rodriguez, found access faithfully, expeditiously and successfully and delivered Columbus' epistle of the friar to the queen. Isabella had already been favorably disposed to Columbus' proposition. She had also received a letter of recommendation from the Duke of Medina Celi at the close of Columbus' late negotiation with him. In 14 days, she wrote back asking Juan Perez to come to the court, giving Columbus hope.

Before midnight of the day the letter was received, the friar saddled his mule and left privately for the court. Through the conquered countries of the Moors, he rode to Santa Fe. The queen admitted him and he pled Columbus' case with characteristic enthusiasm, speaking of Columbus' professional knowledge and experience, his honorable motives, and his capacity to fulfill the undertaking. He also spoke of the solid principles upon which the undertaking was founded, the advantage that must attend its success and the glory it must shed on the Spanish Crown.

Isabella had probably never heard such honest zeal and impressive eloquence. She was more easily influenced than the king and was moved. Her favorite, Marchioness of Moya, warmly seconded the support. The queen requested that Columbus again be sent to her, and, aware of his humble plight ordered 20,000 maravedies in florins ($72, or $216 in 1829 dollars) be sent to Columbus. It was enough for his traveling expenses, a mule and decent clothes so that he might appear respectable in court.

The worthy friar delivered the money and a letter into the hands of the Physician Garcia Fernandez, who delivered them to Columbus, who purchased a mule and clothes and set out at once for the camp before Granada.

Upon arrival, and placed in the care of his steady friend Alonzo de Quintanilla, Columbus was in time to witness the memorable surrender of Granada to the Spanish arms. He watched Boabdil, the last of the Moorish kings, sally forth from the seat of Moorish power while the king and queen moved forward in proud and solemn procession to receive the keys. After 800 years of painful struggle, the Moorish crescent flag was completely cast down. The standard of Spain flew from the highest tower of the Alhambra.

The triumph was one of arms, Christianity, and monarchs. It was the salvation and building up of Spain. The most illustrious, the flower of nobility, the most dignified and pious thronged the court, with bards and minstrels and all the retinue of a romantic and picturesque age. The glittering of arms, the rustling of robes and the sound of music and festivity abounded.

Columbus was described as, "A man obscure and but little known followed at this time the court. Confounded in the crowd of importune applicants, feeding his imagination in the corners of antechambers with the pompous project of discovering a world; melancholy and dejected in the midst of the general rejoicing, he beheld with indifference, and almost with contempt, the conclusion of a conquest which swelled all bosoms with jubilee, and seemed to have reached the utmost bounds of desire. That man was Christopher Columbus."

The moment arrived when the monarchs stood ready to attend his proposals. They kept their word to Christopher Columbus. Persons of confidence were appointed to negotiate with him, among them Fernando de Talavera, now with the conquest, Bishop of Grenada. However, at the outset of their negotiation, unexpected difficulties arose. So fully imbued with the enterprise, Columbus would listen to nothing less than princely conditions.

How does this apply to Extreme Leadership skills?
Answer: An Extreme Leader will face ups and downs. If ups and downs are accepted as a necessary part of the process and the leader maintains resolve and persistence, the door will remain open for success.

Columbus Negotiates

His principal stipulation was that he would be invested with the titles and privileges of Admiral and Viceroy over the countries he should discover, and one tenth of all gains either by trade or conquest. The courtiers who heard his proposals were indignant at such demands. Their pride was shocked to see one considered to be a needy adventurer aspiring to rank and dignities greater than their own. One observer said he was secure at all events of the honor of command and had nothing to lose in case of failure.

To this Columbus replied that he was offering to furnish $1/8^{th}$ of the cost on condition of enjoying $1/8^{th}$ of the profits. His terms were deemed inadmissible. Fernando de Talavera had always considered Columbus a dreaming speculator or a needy applicant for bread. To see a man who for years had been indigent and threadbare as a solicitor in his antechamber, assuming so lofty a tone and claiming an office that approached to the awful dignity of the throne, astonished and made the prelate indignant.

He argued to Isabella that it would be degrading to the dignity of the crown to lavish such distinguished honors upon a nameless stranger. Such terms, she observed, even in the case of success would be excessive, but in the case of failure would reflect badly on the crown.

Isabella, always attentive to her advisers, thought the proposed advantages might be purchased at too great a price. More moderate conditions were offered to Columbus, presented as being highly honorable and advantageous. The positioning of their offer was all in vain; he would not cede one point in his demands and the negotiation was broken off. One must admire Columbus' great constancy of purpose and loftiness of spirit.

> **How does this apply to Extreme Leadership skills?**
> Answer: An Extreme Leader will not shy away from the fundamental purposes behind the Big Vision and will not sell the value of the success of the Big Vision on the cheap.

After 18 Years Columbus Gives Up

More than 18 years had elapsed since Columbus' first correspondence to Paolo Toscanelli of Florence. During that period, what poverty, neglect, ridicule, time consumed in applications to various courts had he suffered. Nothing, however, could shake his perseverance, nor make him descend to terms that he considered beneath the dignity of his enterprise. He forgot his present obscurity and indigence. His ardent imagination realized the magnitude of the contemplated discoveries and his negotiation about empire.

Columbus was so indignant at the repeated disappointments he had experienced in Spain that he determined to abandon his efforts there forever, rather than compromise his demands. Taking leave of his friends, he mounted his mule and left Santa Fe in February 1492 on his way to Cordova, from where he intended to depart immediately for France. When his few zealous believing friends saw his clear intent, they determined to make one last bold effort to avert the loss of Columbus and his plan.

Luis de St. Angel, receiver of the ecclesiastical revenues in Aragon, accompanied by Alonzo de Quintanilla, obtained an immediate audience with the queen, who now supported Columbus warmly in all his solicitations. The urgency of the moment gave St. Angel courage and eloquence. He expressed his astonishment that a queen who had undertaken so many great and perilous enterprises should hesitate at one where the loss could be so trifling while the gain might be incalculable.

He reminded her of how much could be done for the glory of God, the exaltation of the church, and the extension of her own power and dominion. What regret, triumph to her enemies, and sorrow to her friends if this enterprise rejected by her should succeed for some other power. He reminded her of the fame and dominion other princes had acquired by their discoveries, and here was an opportunity to exceed them all. He entreated her to not be misled by the assertions of learned men, that the project was the dream of a visionary.

He supported Columbus' judgment, and the soundness and practicality of his plan and argued that even his failure would not disgrace the crown. It was worth the trouble and expense to clear up even a doubt upon a matter of such importance, for it belonged to enlightened magnanimous princes to investigate questions of the kind and to explore the wonders and secrets of the universe. He stated the liberal offer of Columbus to bear $1/8^{th}$ of the expense and informed her that all the requisites for this great enterprise consisted of but two vessels and 300,000 crowns.

The Marchioness of Moya also exerted her influence. The generous spirit of Isabella was enkindled. She declared her resolution to undertake the enterprise. There was still a moment of hesitation. The king looked coldly on the affair, and the royal finances were absolutely drained by the war. How could she draw on an exhausted treasury for an undertaking to which the king was opposed?

While St. Angel trembled, the queen, with an enthusiasm worthy of herself and of the cause, exclaimed, "I undertake the enterprise for my own crown of Castile, and will pledge my jewels to raise the necessary funds." This was the proudest moment in the life of Isabella; it defined her forever as the patroness of the discovery of the New World. St. Angel, to secure the noble decision, assured her majesty that she would not need to pledge her jewels, as he was ready to advance the necessary funds.

She gladly accepted his offer. The funds really came from the coffers of Aragon; the accountant of St. Angel was paid 17,000 florins from the treasury of King Ferdinand. Some years later, the king would, in remuneration of this loan, use part of the gold brought by Columbus from the New World to gild his vaults and ceilings in the grand palace of Saragoza, in Aragon.

The queen dispatched a messenger on horseback with all speed to call back Columbus. He was overtaken two leagues from Granada, at the bridge of Pinos, a mountain pass famous for bloody encounters between Christians and infidels during the Moorish wars. When he got the message, Columbus was hesitant to again subject himself to the delays and equivocations of the court. However, he was informed of the ardor of the queen and the positive response she had given. So he returned to Santa Fe.

How does this apply to Extreme Leadership skills?

Answer: An Extreme Leader must realize that the time may come when giving up seems like the only remaining option. This moment is when the extreme leader does not give up but rather returns once more to take another run at the objectives. This never-say-die attitude is unique to extreme leaders. Whether Columbus fit this or not we can't be sure. There is a principle in selling called the "take away." When a customer is reluctant to buy, if the offer is suddenly withdrawn, often the customer will drop his or her resistance and want to buy. Maybe Columbus knew this strategy.

Columbus Gets His Way

On arriving at Santa Fe, Columbus had an immediate audience with the queen and her kindness atoned for all past neglect, dispelling every cloud of doubt and difficulty. The concurrence of the king was readily attained. His objections were removed by the mediation of various persons including his grand-chamberlain and favorite, Juan Cabrero. But it was primarily through deference to the zeal of the queen. Isabella was the soul of this grand enterprise while the king remained cold and calculating.

Columbus held out as a great opportunity, the propagation of the Christian faith. He expected to arrive at the extremity of Asia, the vast magnificent empire of the grand Khan and to the dependent islands he read of in the writings of Marco Polo. Columbus reminded the majesties of the previous inclination of the grand Khan to embrace the Christian faith, and of the missions that had been sent by Popes and pious sovereigns, to instruct the grand Khan and his subjects in Catholic doctrines.

Columbus saw that the light of revelation might be extended to the remotest ends of the earth. Ferdinand was not swayed by that reasoning. He had made his religion subservient to his other interests and had found in the Granada conquest that extending the sway of the church might be a laudable means of extending his own dominions. According to the doctrines of the day, any nation that refused to acknowledge the truths of Christianity was fair spoil for a Christian invader.

It is probable that Ferdinand was more stimulated by the accounts given by Columbus of the wealth of Mangi, Cathay, and other provinces belonging to the grand Khan, than by any consideration of converting him and his semi-barbarous subjects. Isabella had nobler inducements – she was filled with pious zeal at the idea of effecting such a great work of salvation. When Columbus later departed, he was given letters for the Grand Khan of Tartary.

Columbus' ardent enthusiasm didn't stop here. With open communications with the Crown and his anticipation of the boundless wealth to be realized through discovery, he suggested that the wealth brought back should be dedicated to the pious purpose of rescuing the holy sepulcher of Jerusalem from the power of the infidels. The sovereigns smiled at his imagination but expressed themselves as well pleased with it and assured him that without the funds that they should be well disposed to that holy undertaking.

This was a deep and cherished design of Columbus – recovery of the holy sepulcher was one of the great objects of his ambition; a goal carried through the remainder of his life and solemnly provided for in his will. Columbus felt he was chosen by heaven as the agent to do this.

Juan de Coloma, the royal secretary, drew out articles of agreement with these terms:

1. That Columbus should have during his life and his heirs and successors forever, the office of Admiral in all the lands and continents which he might discover or acquire in the ocean, with similar honors and prerogatives to those enjoyed by the high admiral of Castile in his district.

2. That Columbus should be viceroy and governor-general over all the said lands and continents; with the privilege of nominating three candidates for the government of each island or province, one of whom should be selected by the Sovereigns.

3. Columbus should be entitled to reserve for himself $1/10^{th}$ of all pearls, precious stones, gold, silver, spices and all other articles and merchandise in whatever manner found, bought, bartered, or gained within his admiralty, the costs being first deducted.

4. Columbus or his lieutenant should be the sole judge in all causes and disputes arising out of traffic between those countries and Spain, provided the high admiral of Castile had similar jurisdiction in his district.

5. Columbus might then and at all after times, contribute an eighth part of the expense in fitting out vessels to sail on this enterprise, and receive an eighth part of the profits. Columbus fulfilled this last point with assistance of the Pinzons of Palos and added a third vessel to the armament in the process.

Thus one-eighth of the expense attendant on this grand expedition, undertaken by one of the most powerful nations, was actually borne by the individual who conceived it and who likewise risked his life on its success.

The Sovereigns signed the agreement on April 17, 1492 at Santa Fe in the Vega or plain of Granada. A letter of privilege or commission was issued for Columbus on the 13th.

In the letter, the dignities and prerogatives of Viceroy and governor were likewise made hereditary in his family; and he and his heirs were authorized to prefix the title of Don to their names. The title would later lose all value in Spain. While both sovereigns signed these documents, the separate crown of Castile defrayed all the expense and during her life few persons, except Castilians, were permitted to establish themselves in the new territories.

> **How does this apply to Extreme Leadership skills?**
> Answer: An Extreme Leader maintains enthusiasm throughout. It is the energy of the leader that fuels the teams involved in the mission. This air of confidence, excitement, and enthusiasm drives the teams who must now execute the Big Vision.

Columbus Gets His Ships

The port of Palos de Moguer in Andalusia was fixed as the place where the armament was to be fitted out. The port's inhabitants, due to some misconduct, had been condemned by the Royal Council to serve the crown for one year, with two armed caravels. A royal order was signed on April 30, 1492 commanding the authorities of Palos to have the two caravels ready for sea within 10 days and to place them and their crews at the disposal of Columbus, who was empowered to procure and fit out a third vessel.

The crews of all three ships were to receive ordinary wages of seamen employed in armed vessels and to be paid four months in advance. They were to sail in such direction as Columbus, under Royal Authority, should command, and were to obey him in all things, with merely one stipulation:

that neither he nor they were to go to St. George la Mina, on the coast of Guinea or any other of the lately discovered possessions of Portugal. A certificate of their good conduct, signed by Columbus, was to be the discharge of their obligation of the crown.

The Sovereigns also issued orders to the public authorities and people of all ranks and conditions in the maritime boards of Andalusia, commanding them to furnish supplies and assistance of all kinds, at reasonable prices, for the fitting out of the vessels and penalties were denounced on such as should cause any impediment. No duties were to be extracted and all criminal processes against the persons or property of any individual engaged in the expedition was to be suspended during his absence and for two months after his return.

A home-felt mark of favor, characteristic of the kind and considerate heart of Isabella, was accorded Columbus before his departure from the court. The Queen issued a letter-patent on May 8th appointing Columbus' son Diego page to Prince Juan, the heir-apparent, with an allowance for his support, an honor granted only to the sons of persons of distinguished rank. After delays and disappointments sufficient to reduce an ordinary man to despair, Columbus took leave of the Court on May 12 for Palos.

Let those who are disposed to faint under difficulties, in the prosecution of any great and worthy undertaking, remember that 18 years elapsed after the time Columbus conceived his enterprise, before he was enabled to carry it into effect, that most of that time was passed in almost hopeless solicitation, amidst poverty, neglect, and taunting ridicule, that the prime of his life had wasted away in the struggle, and that when his perseverance was finally crowned with success, he was about 56 years of age. His example should encourage the enterprising to never despair.

Columbus had more than once presented himself at the gates of the convent of La Rabida but now he appeared in triumph. The worthy friar received Columbus with open arms and he was again the friar's guest. The character and station of Juan Perez gave him great importance in the area and he exerted it to the utmost in support of the enterprise. With his zealous friend, Columbus repaired on May 23rd to the church, St. George in Palos.

There the notary public of the place formally read the royal order, in the presence of the alcaldes and regidors and many of the inhabitants, and full compliance was promised. When the nature of the enterprise became known, horror prevailed as the inhabitants considered the ships devoted to destruction. The owners of the vessels refused to furnish them for so desperate a service and the boldest seamen shrunk from such a wild cruise into the wilderness of the ocean.

All the frightful tales and fables that ignorance and superstition are prone to raise were conjured up and circulated by the gossips of Palos, to deter anyone from embarking in the enterprise. Nothing can be a stronger evidence of the bold nature of this undertaking than the extreme dread with which it was regarded by a maritime community, composed of some of the most adventurous navigators of the age.

Notwithstanding the royal order and the promises of the local magistrates, weeks elapsed without anything being done to fulfill the demands. The worthy prior backed Columbus with all his influence and eloquence but it was all in vain. Not a vessel was to be procured. More mandates were issues on June 20th by the Sovereigns ordering the magistrates to press into service any vessels they might think proper, belonging to Spanish subjects, and to oblige the masters and crews to sail with Columbus.

Juan de Penalosa, an officer of the royal household was sent to see that the order was complied with, receiving 200 maravedies per day while occupied with the business, to be extracted from the disobedient and delinquent, together with other penalties expressed in the mandate. Columbus attempted to act upon the letter in Palos and in the neighboring town of Moguer, with little success other than throwing the communities into confusion, altercations and disturbances.

At length, Martin Alonzo Pinzon, a rich and enterprising navigator (previously mentioned) came forth and took an interest in the enterprise.

His understanding with Columbus was unknown but may have included a division of Columbus' profits. Without Pinzon's assistance, fitting out the small fleet with the necessary armament might have been impossible. He and his brother, VincenteYanes Pinzon, likewise a navigator of great courage and ability, who afterwards rose to distinction, possessed vessels and had seamen in their employ.

They also had relatives in Palos and Moguer and great influence in the community. It is believed that they provided the eighth share of the expense that Columbus was bound to advance. They furnished also at least one of the ships and they resolved to take commands and sail in the expedition. The ships were ready for sea within a month after being thus engaged.

Columbus had reduced his requisitions. He ended up with three small vessels. Two were Caravels (light barques), not superior to river or coasting craft of more modern days. They were shown in old paintings as open, without deck in the center, built up high at the prow and stern with forecastles and cabins for crew accommodations. One of the three was decked. The smallness of the ships was considered an advantage by Columbus in a discovery voyage.

They enabled Columbus to run close to shore and to enter shallow rivers and harbors. That such long and perilous expeditions into unknown seas should be undertaken in vessels without decks and that they should live through the violent tempests by which they were frequently assailed, remain among the singular circumstances of these daring voyages.

How does this apply to Extreme Leadership skills?

Answer: An Extreme Leader knows that when the resources have been attained, the really hard work begins. An extreme leader knows how to switch gears from sales person to operator. Many common leaders cannot make this transition effectively and this is how they fail. They can sell the idea but can't deliver it or choose and motivate a team who can.

Ship Owner Sabotage

During the equipping of the vessels, troubles arose. The Pinta together with its owner and people had been pressed into service by the magistrates, under the arbitrary mandate of the Sovereigns – a striking example of the despotic authority exercised over commerce in those times, that respectable individuals should thus be compelled to engage, with persons and ships, in what appeared to them a mad and desperate enterprise.

The owners of the Pinta, Gomez Rascon and Christoval Quintero, showed the greatest repugnance to the voyage and took an active part in certain quarrels and contentions, which occurred. These people and their friends threw obstacles in the way to retard or defeat the voyage. The caulkers did their work in a careless and imperfect manner and, when commanded to do it over, they absconded. Some seamen who enlisted, repented of their hardihood or were dissuaded by their relatives and sought to retract. Others deserted and hid.

Everything had to be done using the most harsh and arbitrary measures, and in defiance of popular prejudice and opposition. By the beginning of August, every difficulty was overcome and the vessels were ready for sea. On the largest one with decks, the Santa Maria, Columbus hoisted his flag. Martin Alonzo Pinzon, accompanied by his brother Francisco Martin, as pilot, commanded the second, the Pinta. The third, the Nina, had latine sails and was commanded by the third brother, VincenteYanez Pinzon.

There were three other pilots, Sancho Ruiz, Pedro Alonzo Nino, and Bartholomeo Roldan. Roderigo Sanchez of Segovia was inspector- general of the armament and Diego de Arana, a native of Cordova, chief alguazil. Roderigo de Escobar went as royal notary, to take official notes of all transactions. There were also a physician and a surgeon together with private adventurers, several servants and ninety mariners, making in all 120 persons.

Columbus confessed himself to the friar Juan Perez and took communion, followed by his officers and crew. A deep gloom spread over Palos at their departure, with everyone having a relative onboard. The seamen's spirits were depressed beyond their fears seeing the tears and dismal forebodings.

> **How does this apply to Extreme Leadership skills?**
> Answer: An Extreme Leader watches for saboteurs along the way. Big Visions attract detractors who would like to be proven right by seeing the project fail. A leader recognizes these people and their tendencies and takes actions to separate them from the execution phases.

Columbus Finally Departs on the Riskiest Venture of that Time

On the morning of August 3, 1492, Columbus set sail on his first discovery voyage. He departed from a small island in front of the town of Huelva, steering in a SW direction for the Canary Islands, from where he intended to strike due west.

On the third day, the Pinta made signals of distress: her rudder was discovered to be broken and unhung. This Columbus surmised to be done through the contrivance of the owners of the caravel, Gomez Rascon and Christoval Quintero, to disable their vessel, and cause her to be left behind. However, Columbus was able to sail her to the Canary Islands and make repairs, although it further delayed his travels.

There is more to the story but we end here with the appreciation for someone with a Big Vision, who persevered for almost two decades and, although he understandably despaired once, accomplished one of the greatest feats of all time.

> Columbus continued to face incredible obstacles on his voyage – especially in maintaining morale, avoiding mutiny, and sustaining his own convictions in his Big Vision. As we all know, he overcame the many obstacles and achieved his amazing vision. He was certainly not an overnight success but he achieved what no one had done before and what no one could ever claim again. He was an extreme leader.

DR. ELISHA KANE, CAPTAIN OF THE ADVANCE

A Case Study of the Essence of Extreme Leadership in Extreme Circumstances

Based on the book
Arctic Explorations in the Years 1853, '54, '55
By
Dr. Elisha Kane

With excerpts, edits, paraphrasing and commentary
By
Charles Patton

Introduction

From as early as the year 1500, France, England and the Netherlands began searching for a shorter sea route to Asia, one faster than sailing around the tips of Africa or South America. The route most sought after was across the northern extremity of the Americas, through the waters north of what is Canada today. This potential route became known as the Northwest Passage and for nearly 400 years, no one knew if those waters could be navigated all the way to Asia. Many would try but no one would succeed in sailing those treacherous waters until 1904-1906 when Roald Amundsen would accomplish it. Many died trying to chart these desolate waters. In the mid eighteen hundreds, scientists still believed that such a sea route would be open year-round. They based this conclusion on the erroneous belief that salt water didn't freeze because ice bergs were composed of fresh water. It was the potential of finding the Northwest Passage that attracted the explorer, Sir John Franklin, to travel to this desolate part of the world in 1845 to chart as much of this area as possible. It was in those frozen waters that Sir Franklin disappeared and the quest began to determine his fate. ("Northwest Passage," n.d.) This is the story of one of the intrepid men who went in search of Sir Franklin.

Dr. Elisha Kent Kane was a medical doctor who had served under Lt. De Haven on the Grinnell Expedition in 1850. The mission of the Grinnell expedition was to discover the fate of Sir Franklin and his men. Sir John Franklin, a Rear-Admiral in the British Royal Navy, had disappeared sometime between 1845 and 1847 with three ships, 24 officers and 110 men in the Arctic while in search of the Northwest Passage. The first Grinnell Expedition failed to find any trace of Sir Franklin's party.

An important characteristic of an extreme leader is that the person has developed a wisdom based on experience, not necessarily under extreme leadership conditions but definitely in the environment under which the extreme circumstance occurs. In this instance, Kane had been on a prior expedition to the Arctic and knew the conditions and the demands it could place on men.

After the first attempt failed, Dr. Kane proposed to, and was approved under special orders by the U.S. Navy, to lead, as ships' captain, a Second Grinnell Expedition in search of Sir John Franklin and men. The expedition was named after Mr. Henry Grinnell because he provided the ship that Dr. Kane would captain, the Advance. The experiences of Dr. Kane, his officers and crew on the second expedition were beyond remarkable; they were extreme.

Departure

In the spring of 1853, Dr. Kane departed on the Advance with eighteen officers, scientists and crew. He would later pick up en route a nineteen year-old Esquimaux named Hans Cristian, as well as a number of Newfoundland and Esquimaux sledge dogs. With this small crew, their sledge teams and their hermaphrodite brig of 140 tons, which had been thoroughly tried in previous encounters with Arctic ice, they sailed for weeks north along the western shore of Greenland. They had several dangerous encounters with icebergs but managed to sail far beyond civilization before being stopped by ice. In early September, after finding a shelter for their ship in a small harbor called Rensselaer Harbor, the ship was frozen into the ice. The sun would disappear below the horizon on October 24th, so they had much work to do to prepare to survive the winter. Their intent was to search for Sir Franklin as weather would permit during the winter but to do so in earnest come early spring.

They planned to survive the winter living much in the fashion that sailors do. They banked the sides of the ship with snow to conserve heat and accordingly stretch their supply of coal. They occupied any spare moments sending out hunting parties, smoking out rats (nearly burning the ship in the process), and operating an observatory for making scientific observations that was also part of their mission.

Their Situation is Bad

But then troubles began. Their dog team, which was critical to their survival, began to lose members to an unknown "rabies-like" disease. The hunting for walrus, seals, hares, and birds became more and more difficult and less and less successful as the winter progressed until only Hans showed any success, and that was rare. Fresh meat was their greatest defense against scurvy. Occasionally, a hunting or search party would get caught out on the ice when it began to crack and move. With temperatures 25 to 50 degrees below zero, they were able to maintain 60 to 65 degrees inside the ship. However, with the temperature limiting their movements, boredom became a serious concern. They built a false bulkhead to reduce the size of the area that would be heated by their stove, creating crowded but efficient conditions. Their venting of the confined area also had problems with fumes, soot and the ever present risk of carbon-monoxide poisoning.

By January, the temperature stayed consistently in the range of 60 to 75 degrees below zero – 100+ degrees below freezing. At these temperatures, all of the chemicals they used for scientific observations froze including oils, naphtha and chloroform. From October through March they saw no sign of the sun. The constant darkness made the men and the surviving dogs despondent as a strange insomnia set in. Puppies were born but they too died from the strange disease. They found that their fuel supply, the coal, was being depleted faster than planned and had to ration it at three buckets per day. They had no more fresh meat and only a barrel of potatoes left. They became reliant on dried foods and bread. All but two men showed the serious effects of scurvy which include the loss of energy, loosing teeth, receding gums, swollen legs and feet, and pallor.

By March, the temperature remained about 40 to 50 degrees below zero but the sun began showing itself at 15 degrees above the horizon for short portions of the day. The spring tides would raise and lower the ship, still trapped in the ice, seventeen feet twice per day. Attempts to move the ship using harnesses for the men, called Rue-Raddies, failed. In late March, as the

105

temperature began to warm to between 40 and 20 below, they began their search for Franklin in earnest. More than once, the search party itself got into trouble from frostbite, exhaustion, and the effects of scurvy and had to be rescued themselves. Men staggering and collapsing in the snow, and delirium and weakness from their sparse and limited diet were becoming far too common.

By April, one man, Jefferson Baker, died. The day before Baker died, lock-jaw seized him and he emitted the most ominous and frightful sounds the ship's physician, Dr, Hayes, had ever heard. As he was nearing death, a man on deck watch reported men approaching the ship. The band that approached made wild gesticulations, tossing their heads and arms, but appeared to be unarmed. They were native Esquimaux and spoke no English. One of Kane's men, Petersen, was brought from his sick bed because he could interpret some of their language.

> Leaders, like others, come with their own bias toward certain people and their processes, not meaning racial stereotyping, but a bias based on perceived differences in approaches, attitudes, and intelligence. In this regard, Kane had formed biases about the uncivilized Native Esquimaux, different from his relationship with Hans, a civilized native. However, a good leader keeps an open mind and Kane, doing so, began to learn from the Esquimaux important lessons of survival.

After a private interview onboard with their leader, Metek, Kane allowed the others into the ship. While at first Kane was fearful of them, he learned gradually that they were somewhat innocent in their behavior, which made them more of a nuisance than a threat. He found them generally a happy group. He would learn that they did not comprehend the idea of possessions or the idea of future. As a result, they would pilfer the ship as readily as they would let Dr. Kane use their dog teams and sledges. They also would consume all the food available on the day they got it, without the thought of conserving any for the future. They embodied the concept of "living in the moment."

Over the next couple months, while carrying out their search for Franklin, Dr. Kane proceeded to observe how the Esquimaux lived – how they dressed, how they hunted, and how they survived in such a harsh climate. Ohlsen, Kane's carpenter, learned how to make lighter and stronger sledges by emulating the Esquimaux designs. They learned by joining their hunting parties, at which the Esquimaux were far more effective. Kane and the others learned to dress as the Esquimaux dressed: in furs from head to toe.

With the sun out 24 hours per day, the men risked and occasionally suffered snow-blindness. As the ice thinned and melted in some areas, the danger of traveling across thin ice with the sledges, which was the only practical route, became far more dangerous and on one trip Kane fell through the ice with his sledge and dogs and just barely escaped with his life. Their searches for Franklin continued but they remained frustrated without finding any sign of such a large party of men.

Handling dogs pulling a sledge was particularly difficult with their leads (leashes) constantly getting tangled, dogs fighting among each other, and the challenges of using an 18-foot long whip to steer a train of dogs. In addition, often the ice broke up and was compressed into ten to twenty foot high vertical blocks that could be traversed only with the use of axes and great exertion. And, even with increased fresh meat and some greens in their diet, the men continued to suffer from scurvy. By June, eleven of the men were sick with scurvy and snow-blindness. One man, Brooks, had to have his foot amputated as a result of the scurvy. On June 5, Dr. Kane sent a search party to the southwest in one last effort to find Franklin before departing, as the ice was due to melt very soon. Hans, who remained healthy, meanwhile brought seals in daily to sustain the men. Petersen was also harvesting handfuls of one-inch high "scurvy-grass" to feed the men.

When the search party returned, without success, one of the men, McGary, was totally blind from the sun. He reported to Kane that at one point, when sleeping in a tent on the ice while their guns were on the sledge, a polar bear stuck his head into their tent. They were able to fend him off but failed to frighten him away using burning papers and matches. One of the men, Hickey, cut a hole in the back of the tent and, fetching a boat-hook, was able to beat the bear back beyond the sledge where upon he was able to secure a gun and dispatch the bear.

As the nearby ice was no longer safe for travel but still held their ship tight, their searches were limited in range and consistently without success. The summer was wearing on but the ice was not breaking up as it normally would or should have. Kane became concerned about their ability to leave as planned. They tried blasting the ice around them, trying to create an opening (lead) in the ice. Their hopes remained primarily on the gales of late August and early September to free their ship, as they were ill prepared in health, food, and fuel to last another winter.

Their Situation Worsens

By mid-August, Kane began to realize the prospects that they would probably not escape the ice this year and would have to suffer through a harder winter than the one before. As a result of his concerns, he reduced the use of fuel to six pounds of wood per day, to conserve what little coal remained. This meager amount allowed coffee twice per day and soup once. The idea of another year of disease and darkness without fresh food and without fuel was described by Kane as "horrible to think of." They did manage to free the ship enough to warp (i.e., move by pulling with ropes) her inside a group of small islands to what seemed would be a better berth. It was then that Kane realized that they would have to meet their enemy, the impending winter, face to face. In spite of the uncertainty, he knew that inaction was not an option.

An extreme leader anticipates as much as possible. Planning ahead, anticipating the worst while expecting the best and conserving for harder times are what a leader does who might experience extreme challenges. Being prepared and being in the right place at the right time is some peoples' definition of being Lucky. Luck can play a role in success in extreme situations.

At this point, a group of men felt that escape by foot to the south was still practicable. Kane had a difficult decision to make. He was convinced they were wrong and that such an attempt would be extremely dangerous. However, he could not expect his associates to be bound to his own conclusions because, by nautical rules, when a ship is hopelessly beset, the master's authority gives way and the crew is permitted to take their own council. None had signed up for a cruise that would last two winters -- on a ship stuck in the Arctic ice.

The Crisis Point

Kane felt that with a half dozen resolute men remaining with the ship their safety would be more secure than if they left this late in the season. He called the officers and men together, made known to them how the situation looked to him, reviewed the hazards they would face trying to trek out, and then gave them 24 hours to deliberate. He told them that at the end of that time, for those who still wanted to go and who would say so in writing with full explanation as to their reasons, he would give them the best outfit he could, a more than abundant share of the remaining stores and his good-bye blessing.

At noon the next day, he further endeavored to show them that an escape to open water could not succeed, that they had duties to the ship and the other men and strenuously asked them to forgo their plans. He did insist that those who go would need to put themselves under the command of the officers who might choose to join them and that they would need to renounce in writing any claims against those who chose to remain. Kane then took roll and eight of the 17 survivors resolved to stay, including Hans the Esquimaux. Dr. Hayes volunteered to Dr. Kane that he should accompany the men who would leave because he felt they would very likely need the assistance of a doctor. Kane then divided the stores liberally, and saw them off as promised on August 28th with a written assurance that should they be driven back that they would receive a brother's welcome. One man, Riley, would return in a few days.

The skills that Kane applied to this challenge are the most important skills for an extreme leader. He took these steps in addressing dissention among his men:

1. He addressed the problem promptly but not with haste. Timing is everything in extreme leadership.
2. He had his own plan, which he sold to those who would stick with him.
3. Rather than trying to hold back dissenters, he allowed them to separate (or in other circumstances might have taken action to separate them involuntarily) and in the process removed the negative influence from those who would continue to support his vision and goals.
4. He solidified his position with those who would remain with him.
5. As soon as the dissenters were gone, he immediately put those remaining to work on the plan, taking their minds off the negative and on to the positive.

Adapt or Die

The remaining men were now driven to the wall and as such were quickened in their energies and not depressed. Kane immediately went through his plans with them to make certain they were in agreement and then got them to implementing the plans and getting to work. He said there was "nothing like emergency to speed, if not instruct, the energies." Kane directed that their organization and its routine should be adhered to strictly. He was convinced that systematic action was essential to combat difficulties and guide them to improved morale. He laid out duties, schedules and assignments.

He also had learned from the Esquimaux and immediately set upon following more closely their practices of how they lived, what they ate, and how they dressed. He turned an 18 square foot area of the interior of the brig into an igloo, packing turf and moss, an excellent insulation, from floor to ceiling. He figured that the smaller area would be warmed by their body heat and less fuel would be needed. He had the men caulk the floor with plaster of Paris and common paste and covered it with Manila oakum several inches deep, topped with a canvas carpet. He created an entrance, like an igloo, of a low moss-lined tunnel with doors and curtains to close it up. With men sick with scurvy and temperatures dropping again below zero, the work became very hard but it went "bravely on." They gathered enough moss to cover their roof (deck above) and began stripping off the outer-deck planking and stacking it for firewood.

By September, a year since they were first frozen into the ice, wild game was beginning to disappear. An effort to hunt seals like the Esquimaux resulted in Kane's crashing through the ice and nearly being drowned. As it was, he had to abandon a sledge, a kayak they had built, his tent, guns, snow-shoes and everything else he had brought. To keep from freezing to death, he had to run 12 miles back to the brig with Hans "frictioning" him as he ran.

At the brig, problems with the native Esquimaux continued to plague them. Kane considered what the Esquimaux considered "sharing" as theft because the articles, such as cooking vessels and a lamp, where critical to their survival. Kane felt he needed to send a message to the Esquimaux elders so he dispatched two men, Morton and Reilly, to overtake the thieves and bring them back to the brig for punishment. It was a 30 mile trek each way but no one complained. He placed the thieves, Myouk, his wife Sievu, and Aningna, wife of Marsinga, in the brig's hold. He then sent Myouk with a message to their chief, Metek, at the village called Etah, demanding a ransom.

> An extreme leader knows when to draw the line. Understanding, cooperation, and accommodation can only go so far. Sometimes, a stand must be taken regardless of the potential risk. An extreme leader knows where that line is and has a plan to deal with those who cross once too often.

After five days, the chief arrived with another elder, Ootuniah, with a sledge-load of misappropriated items: knives, tin cups, scraps of wood and iron, and other pilfered things. Having not seen guns before the ship's arrival, the natives had become afraid of their "fire-death." Metek admitted to Kane that they thought their "strength" was leaving them when the contingent of men went south. Kane proposed a treaty. Metek agreed that they would no longer steal, would bring them fresh meat, sell or lend them dogs whenever wanted, as long as they weren't in use on a hunt, and show them where to find game. In return, Kane promised to not "visit" them with the "fire-death" or use sorcery on them nor do any hurt. Kane agreed to shoot for them on hunts, welcome them on board the brig, and to seal the deal gave Metek presents of needles, pins, two kinds of knives, a hoop, three bits of hard wood, some fat, an awl, and some sewing thread. Metek gave Kane an allotment of walrus and seal-meat of the first quality. This treaty thereafter was never broken.

From that point forward, their dogs were common property and food was shared by the Esquimaux even when they were themselves starving. They provided the men with supplies of meat at critical periods and became very close allies and even friends.

Throughout the winter, the men who were healthy made long treks as far as 160 miles with dogs along the flat ice along the shore to hunt. They also succeeded in raising the Advance above the line of floatation so that she wouldn't be crushed by the weight of the ice at spring low tides. With the carpenter, Ohlsen, Kane calculated that they could burn seven or eight tons of fuel cut away from the brig without destroying her seaworthiness. Kane figured that they could make it through if they limited their fuel consumption to 70 pounds per day. They cleaned and reconfigured the stove's smoke tubes and ice-melting pans into a more efficient system for warming and melting.

In late October, Erebus, one of the black dogs that were given to the men who had left, returned to the brig. The men surmised she must have broken loose. In the meantime, Hans and Morton tracked the Esquimaux to the lower village of Etah. They brought back 270 pounds of walrus and a couple of foxes, which, with the remaining meat of two bears, would have to last them until daylight returned. The lack of fresh meat would waste them severely. Wilson, Brooks, Morton, and Hans were all on their backs, leaving six to do the work for all. Soon Hans would be back on his feet but Goodfellow would go down.

Kane was amazed at the abilities of the Esquimaux to predict the course of bird migrations based on the conditions of the ice and winds, their knowledge of the habits of the resident animals and the exact range of open water far from where they resided. They could even find, in the frozen darkness, sources of liquid fresh water by tapping the ice with an ice pole and applying their ears to the surface.

In late November, Hans and Kane were out checking traps, in the dark, when a bear came upon their scent. They were unarmed and could hear the bear close by. They were on the ice foot about 10 feet above the flow-ice so Kane told Hans to run for the ship and he would play decoy. Kane knew if they both ran it would incite the bear to chase them. Hans took off like a deer. Kane lay quietly for a few minutes listening for the bear. Peering over the edge of the ice onto the ice flow below, in the dark Kane could not distinguish a bear from the ice-hummocks until one hummock moved, roared and charged. Kane took off as fleet of foot as he had ever run and started throwing off his mittens, hoping to distract the bear with their scent. He made it to the brig where Hans was already advancing with Kane's Marsten rifle. They retraced Kane's footprints and found only one of the gloves and no bear.

In early-December, Esquimaux arrived with five sledges carrying two of the men who had left the brig months before. The two men, Bonsall and Petersen had left the balance of the party 70 miles away, as they said: "divided in counsel, their energies broken and their provisions nearly gone." Only Kane, McGary and Hans were in condition to travel, so Kane organized a rescue party. First he packed up 350 pounds of food with some drink (tea) and dispatched the supplies immediately, reluctantly trusting the Esquimaux to carry them to the stranded men. He did not trust the self- interest of the particular Esquimaux doing the transport so he then prepared Hans to follow their track the next day to ensure the supplies reached their destination. With so many sick, he could not spare another man.

In a mere four days, the Esquimaux returned with the men. With the temperature at 50 degrees below, the men arrived covered with rime and snow and fainting from hunger. Kane welcomed them back as promised, immediately sharing meat-biscuit soup, molasses, wheat bread, and salt pork. They had traveled 350 miles, living solely on limited rations of frozen seal and walrus meat.

> An extreme leader does not hold grudges but rather maintains an open mind. An extreme leader is also cautious of not being taken advantage of and being able to distinguish honest repentance from manipulation and deceit. This is where leadership wisdom comes into play. Experience with people, good and bad, builds on an ability to distinguish those who should be forgiven for their mistakes from those who should be driven away. We are not on earth to judge a person's worthiness before God but we certainly have every right to judge others when it comes to allowing them to be around us.

Kane learned from the Esquimaux that the men, in transit, stopping and being welcomed at huts along the way, had appropriated certain articles of clothing, fox skins and the like, using their superior force. Kane felt this was a form of disrespect and considered the use of fear as being improper given the pact he had formed with the Esquimaux. He held an informal hearing on the matter and as a result returned the articles to them along with five needles, a file and a stick of wood. The Esquimaux were very satisfied. Kane then fed everyone a large dinner and all fell asleep around the stove.

Because of the impact of the crowding on the air quality in their small room, Kane moved four lamps to the area outside their room and put a watch on them. The watch fell asleep and the lamps started the walls of their room on fire, as well as the bulkhead, dry timbers and even the skin of the brig. Because Kane had diligently kept a hole open in the ice for just such an event, by passing buckets of water from outside and using furs brought by the returning men, they were able to put out the fire before the entire room and ship burned to the water line. In fighting the fire, Kane collapsed from the smoke and steam, and when passed up on deck was found to be missing his beard, eye-brows, and forelock and had burns on his forehead and palms. The transition from the fire to the outside, at 46 degrees below zero, was intolerably trying and nearly every man suffered frost-bitten fingers or toes.

Christmas came, with a modest celebration, and then time passed into the New Year, 1855. With 12 lamps constantly going for heat, everything was covered in grease and soot. After a time, the Esquimaux left. Concerned about the atmosphere of smoke and the inhalation of soluble foreign matter, Kane reduced the number of total lamps to four, with two vented to the chimney. Meanwhile, by this time, Kane had lost over 50 dogs to the cursed disease. They had reached the point where the only food available for the remaining five dogs had to be made from a boiled concoction made from the carcasses of the dogs that had died. Only one Newfoundland and three of the Esquimaux dogs remained of the original 50. It was by this time a fearful thing for Kane to think about: taking on a hundred-mile run with dogs that

115

could drop at any moment and leave him stranded in 50-below temperatures but that is what he planned to do in hope of obtaining desperately needed food.

Darkness would continue for months more; total darkness in this area of the Arctic lasted 140 days every year. The men had adapted almost entirely to the ways of the Esquimaux, including relishing a slice of raw blubber, chunk of frozen walrus meat, or walrus liver eaten with little slices of walrus fat. They had come to prefer raw to cooked meat for its taste as well as its ascorbic benefits against scurvy.

One of the men, Wilson, declined in health. Only three men remained healthy – Kane, Hans and Ohlsen. Kane decided it was time for him and Hans to attempt the 93-mile walk in bitter cold and total darkness. Kane saw the choice as stay and lose more men, or attempt the trek and possibly pull the group through until spring. He saw no other choice but to go, but the weather turned severe and he was forced to wait. The temperature hovered between -60 and -40 and at times in the face of severe gale winds. In preparing, Kane would use a lightweight sledge, weighing only 40 pounds, that was as flexible as a "lady's work-basket" with no iron on her, due to its brittleness in severe cold, except along the bottom of the runners. With only four serviceable dogs, the load would have to be light. He and Hans would jog alongside. Kane had learned to dress completely as the Esquimaux did, with a fox-skin jumper called a kapetah, which had a nearly air-tight hood. Beneath the kapetah, he wore another shirt made of bird skins chewed by mouth by the women until it was perfectly soft, with the down next to the body. As many as 500 auks contributed to the making of a single shirt. Britches were made from bear skin or nannooke. Foot gear consisted of a bird-skin short sock with a padding of grass over the sole with the outside being bear skin and wadded with straw. The clothing was loose around the waist and was open to the atmosphere below. In this dress, an Esquimaux will sleep on his sledge in 93 degrees below zero without consequences. The only additional articles were a fox tail held between the teeth to protect the nose from wind and mitts of sealskin well wadded with straw. Esquimaux could be seen with their shirt up scratching their skin in -50 degrees. Kane said, "Our party of American hyperboreans [mythical people living above the north wind] are mere carpet-knights [a soldier who spends his life away from battle] aside of these indomitable savages." To his dress, Kane added layers of wool and fur beneath, without which he could not survive below -50 degrees from his experience.

> Extreme Leaders adapt rapidly to their surrounding circumstances. Lessons must be learned quickly in an emergency and maintaining flexibility to changing circumstances is paramount. Creativity in responding to those changes is also essential and a leader surrounded by trusted advisors is more likely to achieve the creativity needed in crisis. However, caution must be taken to not procrastinate in trying to resolve differences of opinion among advisors. Extreme leaders must use their wits and wisdom to keep action moving in the right direction and in time.

The ice became so thick that the bottom of the ice was grounding out on the bottom at low tide, causing upheaval. Mr. Ohlsen, the carpenter, reported the cross beams were bent six inches, a dangerous level of pressure. Leakage would be disastrous in their condition. In late January, Kane already knew that March would be their critical month. They started burning pieces of tar-laid hemp hawsers to stretch out the supply of firewood and reduced their consumption of wood to 39 pounds per day. Scurvy was worsening with the symptoms of swelling of the limbs, retracting gums, hemorrhaging and horrible despondency. Dr. Hayes' toes needed amputation due to frostbite. Only five men were able to work: Ohlsen, Bonsall, Petersen, Hans and Kane. By the end of January, the weather had still not permitted Kane and Hans to leave for the village of Etah to barter for food.

> An extreme leader takes care of their supporters and will sacrifice their own needs and comforts to ensure the needs and comfort of their supporters are taken care of first. If glory is to be had, an extreme leader shares that glory with their followers but if failure occurs, the extreme leader takes full responsibility of the outcome and never places blame on the followers.

Finally, on February 4th, Kane sent Petersen and Hans south. Ohlsen had collapsed, leaving only Kane and Bonsall on their legs. Kane had to give up trapping due to lack of meat for bait. Any water sitting below a level of two feet off the floor would freeze in their cabin. Four days later, Petersen and Hans returned without reaching Etah because Petersen had broken down with scurvy. Their return allowed Hans and Kane time to hunt and they killed two rabbits which gave the men their first fresh meat in 10 days. By mid-February, Hans' rabbit hunting success picked up. Kane knew that if Hans's health were to fail, they all would be lost. Kane felt optimistic that, with continued hunting by Hans, they would be able to contain the scurvy. He also believed that the coming of the sun would help morale and, as long as they stayed alive, they would stick together. A week later, Hans shot a deer yielding 180 pounds of meat but unfortunately it putrefied rather quickly and most was lost.

By early March, the sun began to peek above the horizon. Kane finally but reluctantly sent Hans off to the village of Etah – the 93-mile trip, expecting him back in four to five days. In four days, he in fact did return and reported the settlement was in a state of famine. They had even eaten 26 of their 30 dogs. Hans was able to shoot a walrus for them while he was there. Hans returned with his share of the meat and brought an Esquimaux, Myouk, who Kane had asked him to bring to help with the hunting.

Desertion Cannot Be Tolerated
By mid March, they had burned the last of the Manila hawser so Kane had Petersen strip off more wood from the brig. Kane also got wind of a possible

desertion by two men who were planning to steal the sledge and dogs from Hans. The consequences would be fatal to the sick men so Kane knew he must deal with them. He confronted them, put a stop to it and punished the perpetrators. However, one, Godfrey, escaped and headed south on his own. Kane worried that Godfrey would head to Etah and steal Hans' sledge and dog team. Kane would have left immediately to pursue him but was unable to do so because the sick needed a constant supply of food.

> An extreme leader takes whatever action is necessary to protect their followers. Threats to the health and wellbeing of followers must be dealt with firmly and promptly, regardless of the risk. Under-miners must be removed as quickly as discovered even at the expense of progress in the short term.

By late March, Kane could not help but compare their current condition to their condition a year ago. They had learned to adapt well but the condition of the men was much farther deteriorated. To cut away two days worth of fuel from the brig took them a full day. Godfrey and the danger he might pose for Hans kept weighing heavily upon Kane's mind but the condition of his men kept him from taking action himself.

On April 2nd, a man was reported near the brig and Kane went to investigate. Leaving Bonsall behind, armed and on the deck, he located the man among the hummocks. It was Godfrey. Seeing Kane apparently unarmed, Godfrey allowed Kane to approach. He did not know Kane had a concealed pistol. Kane drew it and was able to force Godfrey back to the ship but he refused to board. Kane left him under the guard of Bonsall and went below for irons. As soon as he reappeared, Godfrey bolted. Bonsall's weapon failed at the cap. Kane went for the gun rack but his first rifle choice went off in the act of cocking. A second aimed in haste missed the mark. Godfrey made good his escape. On further investigation, Kane discovered near the ship the sledge and dogs that Godfrey had originally stolen and on the sledge an amount of walrus meat, which Kane considered a godsend that that moment. Godfrey had inadvertently done more good than harm.

Kane was now firm in his believe that Godfrey was dangerous. Hans had been gone over two weeks when normally he would only be gone four to five days. Kane felt it necessary to issue an order to the remaining men that any further act of desertion would be met with the sternest penalty, meaning death. Kane's concern for Hans grew to the point where he knew someone would have to go in search of his trusted friend and because of the condition of the men, knew it would have to be him.

On April 10th, Kane left with five dogs, the smallest sledge and the lightest load possible. Being, as he described it, more than half Esquimaux, all he took on the sledge was an extra jumper and sack pants for sleeping and a frozen ball of raw walrus meat packed with tallow shaped into a twisted form he could break off with a stone. After covering 64 miles in 11 hours, Kane saw a small speck ahead of him on the ice that he soon recognized from his familiar gait as Hans. In 15 minutes they were jabbering in a patois of Esquimaux and English. Hans had fallen ill and was down for five days. Nearby was a broken down stone hut at a place called Anoatuk which had in the past provided shelter from severe storms. Even though the weather was tolerable, they settled there to enjoy some tea and molasses that Kane had brought in a small jar in his pocket because he knew it was a favorite of Hans. Hans carried a few lumps of walrus liver which they also shared. Hans shared also that, before falling ill, he had hunted successfully with the Etah Esquimaux and had stashed his share of the meat on a nearby island. Hans told also how, after falling ill, he had been nursed back to health by the young daughter of one of the elders, Shunghu. Kane sensed that she may have touched Hans' heart.

Hans told Kane how Godfrey had tried to talk him into traveling south with him and when he refused tried to steal his rifle but Hans had overpowered him. Hans told Kane that Godfrey then proposed taking some of Hans' walrus meat back to the ship with the "viewing of making terms" with Kane. Kane figured Godfrey was trying to link up with the man who had planned to follow Godfrey but had been detained from doing so. Kane firmly believed that he had to capture Godfrey and to return and confined him on the brig for the safety of all concerned.

Kane sent Hans to a lower Esquimaux settlement, near Cape Alexander, to negotiate for four dogs. He authorized Hans to offer in return his remaining dog team when they finally headed south. Kane realized that if the ice again did not melt, he must be prepared to move south without his ship. He committed to himself to make a final decision in early summer when they would still have time.

April 12th found Kane back at the brig. The men were again without fresh food until Hans arrived with rabbits and a walrus liver. Kane had become more and more like the Esquimaux, having adapted their attitude of "The day provides for itself; or, if it does not, we trust in the morrow, and are happy till tomorrow disappoints us." Hans had failed in his efforts to negotiate for additional dogs but had brought back two Esquimaux, Metek and one of his nephews, to help with hunting. Metek told Kane that the winter had been hard on the Esquimaux; that even bands of Esquimaux from farther south had traveled north in search of food. They ended up having to kill many dogs to survive. Kane estimated that the eight known settlements of Esquimaux including about 140 members had no more than 20 dogs remaining. Besides natural deaths, three murders and an infanticide had further depleted their numbers. The tribes themselves admitted to numbers that indicated to Kane that they were dying out, progressing rapidly toward extinction. But, when Kane explained this to them, they just laughed.

Kane hatched an idea to recapture Godfrey. He traded places with the nephew and, dressed like him, accompanied Metek back to his village at Etah. His trick worked. When the village population turned out to greet their returning leader, Godfrey was among them. Kane was able to get right up next to him and place his pistol to his ear before he knew Kane was there. Kane put Godfrey into the irons he had brought with him. They remained overnight with Metek and his family and in the morning Kane transported Godfrey to the brig.

A week later, Kane again sent Hans on a mission to borrow dogs, sending with him an iron bar suitable for making harpoon shafts as currency to help in the transaction. In about a week, Hans returned well laden with Walrus meat and accompanied by three Esquimaux each with a sledge and dog team, equipped for a hunt. The party leader, Kalutunah, was a noble savage, as Kane described him. Kane sat with him and proposed one last closing expedition as far north as they could travel.

Within a couple of days, the three Esquimaux, Kane and Hans departed. They searched a large area, traveling until early May. They found no sign of Sir Franklin but they did observe vistas never before seen by non- Esquimaux and recorded for posterity new valleys, capes and harbors. Kane also got to witness how Esquimaux attacked and killed a polar bear with only lances and knives. He described that five of every seven Esquimaux are scarred by direct teeth wounds from bears.

While preparations for departing had been in progress as energies permitted for over nine months, after Kane returned from his final search, efforts intensified.

> When a plan hasn't worked and a radical change in direction is needed, an extreme leader doesn't hesitate to make the change. Solid planning for the alternative is essential because failing a second time would be devastating to morale and would cost continued support of followers. Even when the failure is from no fault of the leader or followers, it is essential to not fail a second time. Followers will understand one failure but a second, not so readily.

Abandoning Ship is Never Easy

It was clear to Kane that the brig could not be saved and would need to be abandoned. His primary plan that he laid out to his men consisted of loading the brig's three boats with only the most essential equipment, food supplies and the sick and then pushing and pulling them across jumbled and dangerous ice, filled with tall hummocks, cracks winding for miles and gale force storms to the closest location of open water – hundreds of miles to the south. They would build runners on the bottom of the three boats to make it easier for the weakened men to move the boats, named: "Faith," "Hope," and, oddly, "The Red Boat."

For food, they took ships' bread pounded into powder, pork fat and tallow melted down and frozen, a stock of concentrated bean soup that was also frozen and put into bags, and the remaining supply of flour and meat-biscuit sewn into double bags to protect from moisture. For meat, they would rely on their guns and hunting along the way.

They held a memorial upon leaving the ship but, as it turned out because their travel across the ice was slow and tedious, many trips were made back to the brig to cook and to secure various items determined later to be needed. During the memorial, all men signed a document placing them under the command of Dr. Kane. Dr. Kane also signed a letter attesting to the fact that the brig could not be saved. With few provisions remaining, the mission of finding Sir Franklin could no longer be performed and any further cutting of firewood would make the ship unseaworthy. Wintering in the brig another year was not an option.

> An extreme leader will recognize the sacrifices of others at every opportunity. Even abandonment of a failed effort can be an opportunity to celebrate. Kane considered the Advance to be a member of their family in that it sheltered and protected them through two harsh winters and gave up its life for them. It deserved some respect on leaving her behind.

Putting every possible available man who could stand to the task, he assigned six men to move each boat. With only 12 healthy men, they could only move two of the three boats at a time. Kane had done some early work in anticipation and went ahead of the boats to set up a "field hospital" in the hut at Anoatuk where the ill would rest and avoid much of the rugged travel. He then traveled back and forth to transport each of the four ill men to the comfort of the hut. In doing so, Kane saved them from the exposure to the elements the other men had to endure. Kane believed the hut saved the lives of the ill men, giving them additional time to recover and because it gave them a change of scene, it improved their morale. He also had by this time reincorporated Godfrey into the work team, as he was displaying an acceptable degree of trustworthiness.

Kane dispatched Godfrey to Etah to try to obtain meat. He returned with the meat as expected and brought with him Metek, who pitched in to help. In testament to the difficulty of this undertaking, after 14 hours, the weakened men had moved the boats over 12 miles of surface but had advanced all of a mile and half from their starting point, the brig.

Kane repeatedly traveled back to the brig to bake bread, raising it in three hours without salt, baking soda or shortening (a mysterious achievement that he doesn't explain). In total, Kane and his men moved 1,500 pounds of provisions from the brig to the boats, which may sound like a lot but they were consuming under their heavy exertion more than 100 pounds per day, including the dogs.

When Kane began moving provisions to Etah, he found the ice turning sodden and it could no longer be trusted. Kane began to worry about what might happen if any of their critical supplies were lost. When he reached Etah, he found all the inhabitants gathered upon a single large rock, laughing and enjoying a feast on auks which had returned in great numbers to roost in the rocks above them. He noticed that they thought nothing of the next winter but simply ate what they caught. Kane exchanged dog teams with them, as theirs were now well fed. An elder provided Kane with a sledge full of walrus meat and sent two young men to join him to assist him through a nearby section of broken ice. Before he left, he marveled at the careless play of the children and the ordinary life they seemed to enjoy in the most unordinary place on earth. It pained him to think of the winters they would endure year after year. The families lived as one big family. Their villages were spaced apart at the length of a day's dog-march and were located where hunting was known to be good. So familiar were their routes that their dogs knew where to go almost without guidance. The Esquimaux had named every change in season, every rock, every plant and every safe place to cache meat. Kane believed that while they had no special resistance to exposure and fatigue, being no more capable than a well-trained outsider, they had vast knowledge of the dangers that surrounded them and knew how to deal with dangers from which Non-Esquimaux would shrink.

> An extreme leader works as hard if not harder and sacrifices as much if not more than what that leader asks others to do. This is the sign of a true leader as well as an extreme one. Leaders do not place themselves above those who follow. That distinction is what earns a leader the respect needed to maintain the position of authority.

When Kane returned to the boats, a strong storm had driven the men to turn the boats over and crawl under them. Their appetites continued strong, consuming more than three pounds of food per day per man. Kane decided to return to Etah with Petersen and ask for more Esquimaux to come and help move the boats. They departed in the face of one of the most fearful gales he had ever experienced – of cyclone force. It was such a fierce storm that at times he, Petersen and the dogs had to lie flat on the ice to keep from being blown away. It became so intense that they lifted the sledge on their shoulders and ran with it for the shelter of the rocks of a small island, and after exhausting exertions, reached firm ground. They were safe from the unpredictable movements of the ice but not out of danger. They could not keep their feet and the air was so thick with snow that it was as dark as night even though it was the full daytime of summer. Kane and Petersen could not see each other or the dogs. They found no ledge or knob on the island to give them refuge. Kane made the decision that they had to make for the mainland across the dangerous ice, which they did. Reaching the shore they found the shore was rock, thirty feet high, with drifts piled up against them. They barely had the energy to dig a burrow and drag the dogs with them into the snow drifts. More snow soon piled over them as the storm raged outside. Their fur jumpers had been blown off their backs by the wind and with the combined warmth of their bodies and respiration they were soon wet to the skin. At that point, one of the dogs began to have a fit which instigated a dog fight. Only with great effort was the conflict mediated but in the process the canopy over their heads collapsed exposing them again to the fury of the elements. Never at sea had Kane ever experienced such noise and tumult. The snow drifted over them again and they waited. Finally, Kane decided that proceeding against the storm was impossible but they might use the storm to their advantage, keeping it to their backs, to return to the boats on the ice, which they did, reaching them in 20 hours, while covering only 40 miles.

They suffered several accidents with boats falling through the ice, but in one the "Faith" was nearly lost. In a valiant effort to save it, Ohlsen, a very powerful man, grabbed a capstan-bar and used it to arrest the sinking boat and in the process lost his balance, requiring even a more desperate effort to the point that he injured himself and within three days died. His heroic efforts saved the boat and potentially the lives of his comrades.

At one point, they were able to raise sails on the boats and sail them across a stretch of flat ice, making the distance in one day equal to the previous five. Soon the two leaders from Etah arrived with Kane's dogs, now all recovered. He dispatched the combined set of dogs with a sledge to retrieve the sick from the hut at Anoatuk and bring them to Etah. In another week, five men and two women arrived from Etah to help. Even with the added help, the boats continued to periodically break through the ice.

Kane had not seen Hans for two months. Hans had asked Kane to allow him to go south on the mission to replace his boots and lay in a stock of walrus hide for soles. He said he would walk so as to not tie up the dogs. Kane gave him permission expecting to see him again in three to four weeks. Then, with all their labor, he hadn't thought much about Hans until he realized he had been missing for so long. From making inquiries of the Etah Esquimaux, Kane learned that Hans had stopped by Etah and arranged for the leather but then went across the big headland to a village called Peteravik where Shanghu and his pretty daughter lived. Kane never saw him again but heard he had traveled south to another principality high up Murchison's Sound, a married man.

Another accident with the ice almost lost the Red Boat with all the documents of the voyage with it. The loss of all their logs and scientific recordings would have been a severe blow to their morale. Again, by extreme efforts on the part of Morton, everything was saved but only after Bonsall grabbed Morton by the hair as he sank below the icy water after securing the boat.

They finally reached Etah and, after feeding on auks and a brief celebratory visit, they pushed their boats to the edge of the ice, where open water could be seen extending to the horizon. They launched their three boats with fair goodbyes and sailed onto the open water as tiny specks upon an iceberg-filled and treacherous sea. They sailed, rowed, got stuck numerous times in the ice, and had a last chance with their last bullet to shoot a seal desperately needed to keep them from starvation. After 84 days at sea in small boats, they reached the northernmost non-Esquimaux settlement, Upernavik, a Danish colony. It would be their first encounter with civilization in three years.

The men had a very hard time adjusting to the heat of indoors and, in the midst of a reception thrown in their honor, the host found them sitting outside on piles of snow. The adjustment back from the life lived as Esquimaux took more than a little time. Kane also managed to bring back two dogs, which he had carried in the boats as "meat on the hoof" but, having become attached to them, he had put off killing them for food to the very end. They had managed to reach civilization before their time had come.

One, Toodla, had saved his life when he and the sledge had fallen through the ice and he was attached to the big girl.

Kane brought back 15 of the 18 who had ventured north with him, an admirable result considering what they had lived through.

What happened to Sir Franklin and his men was never totally determined. Some evidence of encampments, the sinking of their ships and a few graves were found but what had become of the larger body of men was never discovered. The full story of their disappearance remains a mystery to this day.

Conclusion

In summary, the essence of extreme leadership is to be the leader, have a vision and set the goals that support the vision, involve the team of followers in developing the plans to achieve the goals, set the example in work ethic and hardship, delegate the right assignments to the right team members, respond intelligently when crises arise, not dawdle on urgent matters, use the wisdom gained from experience to make the right decisions, remove any dissenters or under-miners as soon as possible, get the team to work on the plans they helped devise as soon as possible, monitor the team's progress regularly, adapt and be flexible as circumstances change and setbacks happen, take tough action against threats, take better care of the team than the leader takes care of him or herself, and share the glory, when there is glory to be shared, and take all the blame when setbacks or failures occur. And, admit mistakes when mistakes are made. A team knows when their leader is being less than honest so truthfulness with everyone is the best practice. Protecting the team's trust at all times is critical. These are the skills of a great leader in extreme circumstances.

What was Gandhi's Big Vision? His Big Vision was his idea that civil disobedience could be used to change or eliminate morally wrong statutory enactments without violence.

MAHATMA GANDHI

A Case Study of an Extreme Leader with Commitment,
Determination and Persistence

Based on the Autobiography
The Story of My Experiments with Truth
By Mahatma
Gandhi And other
sources

With excerpts, edits, paraphrasing and commentary
By
Charles Patton

His Early Life (Indian Child, p. 1)

Born on October 2, 1869 in Porbandar, India, Mohandas Karamchand Gandhi became one of the most respected spiritual and political leaders of the 1900s. He was heavily influential in freeing the Indian people from British rule through the novel approach of nonviolent resistance and is honored by Indians as the father of the Indian Nation. He was called Mahatma by the Indian people, meaning Great Soul, later by the name of reverence, Gandhiji. He was married through a parental arrangement at the age of 13 to a girl the same age. He had four children, studied law in London and returned to India in 1891 to practice law. In 1893, he took on a one-year contract to do legal work in South Africa, at the time under British control. When he attempted to claim his rights as a British subject, he was abused and soon saw that all Indians suffered similarly. He worked in South Africa for 21 years to secure rights for Indian people.

His Big Vision

He led the campaign for Indian independence from Britain, based on the principles of courage, non-violence and truth, a method of civil disobedience that he called Satyagraha – withdrawing cooperation from the state. He was arrested many times by the British for his activities in South Africa. He believed it honorable to go to jail for a righteous cause. He spent seven years in prison, off and on. He often fasted to impress upon others the need to be nonviolent.

Influenced by this philosophy, large masses of followers began to boycott British education institutions, law courts, and products; to resign from government employment; to refuse to pay taxes; and to forsake British titles and honors. Gandhi sought to have oppressors and the oppressed alike recognize their common bonding and humanity.

His Challenges

His strategy was not without setbacks.

What obstacles did he have to overcome? He was forced to call off a campaign in protest to the British occupancy in 1922 because of atrocities committed by his supporters against police. He was imprisoned and remained so until 1925.

After his release from prison, he set up a commune and a newspaper and inaugurated a series of reforms aimed to help the socially disadvantaged, the rural poor, and the untouchables. He continued with these efforts until 1930.

In 1930, he emerged again to lead a 400 km (248 mile) march in a protest against extortionist British taxes on salt. He and thousands of followers illegally but symbolically made their own salt from seawater. Their defiance reflected India's determination to be free, despite the imprisonment of thousands of protestors. As a result of this defiance, for the next five years, the congress struggled to put into law a complex agreement that would represent all the people of India. In February 1937, provincial autonomy became a reality.

India was granted independence in 1947. Gandhi had been an advocate for peaceful coexistence between Hindus and Muslims but when the British partitioned India and Pakistan, bloodshed between the two religions broke out. On January 13, 1948, at the age of 78, he began a fast with the purpose of stopping the bloodshed between the two factions. After five days of his fasting, the opposing leaders pledged to stop the fighting and Gandhi broke the fast. Twelve days later, a Hindu fanatic, who opposed the tolerance of all creeds and religions, assassinated him.

His Qualifications as an Extreme Leader
Gandhi can be considered an extreme leader on many levels.

What was it that made Gandhi a successful leader? His methods amazed people and endeared him to his followers. The purity of his morals enabled people to hear what he had to say. His actions showed people the way to his vision.

Throughout his life, he was a man of meager means. He did not require fancy surroundings, and in fact, chose the opposite extreme. He epitomized the Extreme Leader characteristic of taking care of others before you take care of yourself. He also took up weaving, seen as woman's work, as a way to symbolically embrace the rights of women and bring those rights into the fabric of society – by crossing the gender lines. He also was never impressed by anyone's title or standing, and never looked beyond each person's simple humanity. He also performed his work on the borders, on the boundaries between people – England and India, Muslims and Hindus, rich and poor.

> Boundaries play a role in extreme leadership. Extreme leaders tend to operate on the boundaries of new discovery, in the area of resolving seemingly impossible disputes and in breaking down the arbitrary boundaries humans so often erect to protect vested interests.

Another characteristic of an Extreme Leader that Gandhi displayed: he was not perfect and did not think of himself that way, although to most he appeared that way.

Additionally, he knew clearly the reward that he sought. Some seek fame and some fortune. In his case, when the independence he sought finally came to the Indian people on August 15, 1947, he was not even present at the celebration festivities in New Delhi because fame and glory were not what motivated him. (http://www.asianwindow.com/india/how- did-mahatma-gandhi-spend-august-15-1947/)

In the end, as often happens to Extreme Leaders, his death was by assassination – shot by a fanatic, who did not believe in religious coexistence, while his hands were still folded in greeting to an audience gathered for a prayer meeting. He blessed his assailant before collapsing. He died on Jan. 30, 1948 at 5:12PM. (Gandhi, 1957, p. 1-560)

A partial summary of Gandhi's observations include

1. All people can shape and guide their lives according to the highest ideals, no matter how insignificant and powerless they might feel themselves to be.

2. Be deeply rooted in your own cultural and religious heritage and remain utterly opposed to all forms of social, ethnic or religious intolerance.

3. Evil means will corrupt and degrade not only the purposes for which they are undertaken but also the persons who stoop to such means.

4. Personal change and the ability to bring about social change are linked to the principles of nonviolence, justice in public affairs, celibacy (in thought as well as deed), and no cooperation. You must practice these principles in your own life first, and then do what you can to encourage society as a whole to adopt them.

5. Individuals can carve out, should they so wish (i.e., commit to), "zones of peace" in their own lives – territories where every effort will be made to banish violence, discord and untruth.

Author's observations drawn from Gandhi's own words in the original biography

- He made sure that every penny was accounted for and for every expenditure a receipt was made and recorded.

- He believed that the heart's earnest and pure desire is always fulfilled.

- He believed that Western Civilization was, unlike the Eastern, predominantly based on force.

- Because he lived under British rule, he felt compelled to participate in the Boer War and, in London during WWII, in the ambulance service, and pursued the independence of India within and through the British Empire.

- He always contacted the opposition leadership to give them a chance to respond before taking action (or imposing non-action) against them.

- He applied wet earth bandages (using "good earth") to patients' heads and chests to cure many ills, including the black plague.

- Civility is the most difficult part of his total philosophy – not the mere gentleness of speech cultivated for the occasion, but an inborn gentleness and desire to do the opponent good. He believed that it should show in every act.

- The actions taken by him and his followers were to first meet with the opposition leaders and present their requests, then they asserted their will, then they stood their ground, then other followers began to support them, then they went to jail, then they fasted. The opposition's reaction was, at first, arrogance, forgetting that civil servants serve the people, not dictate to them. The second reaction was ignoring their request. The third reaction was attempted coercion. The fourth was attempted penalization. Then the opposition resorted to enforcing the law (or taking action not supported by the law). Lastly they caved in to the pressure.

Conclusion

Gandhi had no idea when he started just how his grand his Big Vision would become but he believed it would achieve some results and he felt that even in failure it would do no harm.

HERNANDO CORTES, EXPLORER

A Case Study Showing the Distinction between Purpose and
Leadership Skills
And Examples of Skills Used in Achieving Big Visions

Based on the book
History of the Conquest of Mexico
The Life of the Conqueror Hernando Cortes
By
William H. Prescott

With excerpts, edits, paraphrasing and commentary
By
Charles Patton

Introduction

In reading this example of an extreme leader, note well the distinction between the <u>skills</u> that extreme leaders use and the <u>purpose</u> for which they use them. An extreme leader may use effective leadership skills for either good or bad purposes and examples can be found in history in equal measure from one end to the other on the spectrum of good and evil. In using this example we in no way endorse the actions taken by Cortes in brutalizing the native Aztecs. His actions were akin to the actions taken by the settlers in North America against Native Americans, which many recognize today as having often been cruel, unfair and too often fatal. His actions reflect the outlooks and attitudes in those historic times, as the major political and religious powers sought to claim large portions of the New World using indiscriminate force. The results of Cortes' actions are reprehensible; yet we can still study the methods he used for examples that might apply to more appropriate purposes in our "more civilized" world of today. The message for the reader is that extreme leaders have plied their skills for evil purposes as often as they have for honorable ones. Also, the perception of what is good and what is evil can be different, depending on the leader's focus, and on history's judgment.

Even Cortes believed what he was doing was honorable – in the eyes of his monarchy, his church and his peers and countrymen, he was a Soldier of the Cross. It is only through the eyes of the vanquished and the hindsight of historians that the cruelty he imposed can really be judged. He was described by William Prescott "… as not being cruel, at least not as cruel compared with most of those who followed." He also described Cortes as being "severe in enforcing obedience to his orders for protecting the natives and their property." His directions were not always followed but he would enforce them severely whenever he learned of violations.

> Extreme leaders know their purpose clearly before beginning to apply
> their leadership skills to that purpose. Hopefully, that purpose is for
> good rather than evil.

Cortes' Beginnings (Prescott, 1843, p. 1-467, 1-490)

Cortes was born in Medellin, near Seville, Spain in 1485. His father was an
infantry captain. His father and mother were respected for their excellent
"qualities." In his youth, he was feeble but strengthened as he grew older. At
14 he was sent by his father to Salamanca to be educated in the law. He
showed little fondness for books. After two years, he returned home, to the
great chagrin to his parents. He had learned some Latin and wrote good
prose but otherwise, he was an idler until, at age 17, he proposed to enroll in
the military for the adventurous life it offered.

After deciding on an opportunity to sail under Don Nicolas de Ovando,
successor to Columbus, he fell from a high wall, while accessing a lady's
apartment, received a severe contusion in the process, and, being confined
to bed for a time, missed the fleet's departure. He remained at home two
more years, profiting little.

Off to Sea

In 1504, at age 19, the year Queen Isabella the Catholic died, he sailed with
Alonso Quintero in one ship in a small squadron of vessels bound for the
Indian islands. Quintero tried to sneak off early to Hispaniola, ahead of the
other ships in his group, but ran into and became lost among heavy gales.
Finally, a dove landed on the mast and Cortes took it as a sign of a miracle
when its path led them to Hispaniola. Because of the delays caused by
maneuvering through the storms, Quintero's companions arrived after
Cortes. Upon landing, Cortes went to the house of the governor, the man he
had known in Spain, Don Ovando. The governor convinced Cortes to stay
and receive a grant of land, which he did, in the town of Acua. He settled
there for a time, often spending his time indulged in duels and, though an
expert swordsman, he received numerous scars.

Cortes Becomes a Soldier

He occasionally participated in military actions to suppress native uprisings under Ovando's lieutenant, Diego Velasquez. He became familiar with the tactics, toil and danger of Indian warfare along with the deeds of cruelty that were then practiced.

In 1511, when Velasquez undertook the conquest of Cuba, Cortes abandoned hi s quiet life and joined the expedition. Throughout the invasion, he displayed an activity and courage that won him the attention of the commander; while his free and cordial manners, good humor and lively sallies of wit made him a favorite of the soldiers. He showed little of his later qualities of discipline and seriousness. After the conquest of the island, Cortes seemed to be held in great favor by Velasquez, now governor, who made him his Secretary.

On the island, he became enamored with Catalina Xuarez from Granada, Spain. He apparently gave his promise to marry her but then resisted pressure from the lady's family and the governor to keep his promise after becoming enamored with one of Catalina's sisters, and she with him.

Cortes Crosses the Establishment

Cortes became cold toward the governor and began meeting with others who were discontent over the distribution of lands and offices. The malcontents decided to lay their grievances before the authorities in Hispaniola from whom Velasquez had received his commission.

The voyage to Hispaniola was one of some hazard, in an open boat, across 18 leagues of sea (about 47 miles), and they fixed on Cortes as the fittest man to undertake it. The conspiracy reached the governor's ear before the envoy's departure. The governor seized Cortes, fettered him and placed him in strict confinement. It was said that he would have hung Cortes except for the interposition of his friends. Cortes did not remain long in confinement – he worked himself free and escaped, forcing open a window. He made his way to a church and claimed sanctuary.

The governor, while incensed about the escape, did not want to violate the sanctity of the church. So, he stationed a guard in the area to watch for Cortes to leave. In a few days, it happened. Cortes was standing outside the front walls when the guard suddenly sprang on him from behind and pinioned his arms while others rushed in and secured him. Cortes in New Spain (i.e., Mexico) later hanged this same man, Juan Escudero, for his part in a similar plot against Cortes. Cortes was again put in irons.

He was carried on board a vessel set to sail in the morning to Hispaniola. He was again able to work his feet through the rings of his shackles, went carefully on deck, covered by darkness, and stole quietly down the side of the ship into a boat lying below. He pushed off quietly. As he drew near the shore, the currents became rapid, turbulent and strong. Being an excellent swimmer, he boldly plunged into the water. Struggling for his life, he succeeded in reaching the shore. He went immediately back to the church, again claiming sanctuary.

For some unexplained reason, Cortes relinquished his objections to the marriage with Catalina Xuarez, thus securing the good graces of her family. Soon after, the governor relented on his efforts to confine Cortes.

A strange story is told in connection with this event. It is said that Cortes in proud spirit refused to accept the reconciliation and, leaving his sanctuary, presented himself unexpectedly before Velasquez in his own quarters, while on a military excursion some distance from the capital.

Startled by the sudden apparition of Cortes, his enemy completely armed before him, with some dismay, Velasquez asked the meaning of it. Cortes answered by insisting on a full explanation of the governor's previous conduct. After some hot debate, the interview ended amicably. When a messenger arrived to announce the escape of Cortes, he found Cortes and the governor sleeping together on the governor's bed. The reconciliation was permanent but Cortes was not reinstated as Secretary.

Cortes did receive an allotment of Indians for use as forced labor, called *repartimientos*, along with an ample territory near St. Jago, of which he was soon made Alcalde. He lived almost wholly on his estate, devoting himself to agriculture with more zeal than before. He introduced some new breeds of cattle to Cuba. He started and operated gold mines that promised better returns than the mines on Hispaniola. Within a few years, he had accumulated some 2,000 to 3,000 castellanos, a large sum for one in his situation – at some cost in Indian lives.

The Gold Bug Bites -- Cortes and the Governor

When another Spaniard, Grijalva, returned from Mexico with tidings of discoveries and rich fruits of his traffic with natives, the news spread like wildfire, for all saw in it the promise of more riches than any thus far obtained. The governor resolved to explore the same areas as Grijalva but taking with him considerable armament. He looked for a proper person to share the expense of it and to take command. He rejected one Hidalgo after another. The governor trusted two men and Cortes, who was close with both men, asked them to recommend him as the suitable person to be entrusted with the expedition.

> An extreme leader takes action when opportunity presents itself. An extreme leader also has ambition and is willing to give all to achieve a noble purpose – maintaining intense concentration on the Big Vision.

Cortes is reputed to have offered his recommenders a liberal share of the proceeds of the expedition. They urged his selection with all their eloquence. Cortes had acquired a fortune, and he had the requisite experience to lead the expedition. His popularity would also attract followers to his standard. The governor called for Cortes and announced his intent to make him Captain-General of the Armada. Cortes now had attained the object of his wishes since he had set foot in the New World – to claim Mexico for Spain and the Pope.

Cortes saw boundless potential open to him – no more drudgery being cooped up on a petty island. This was his opportunity to satisfy his cravings of ambition and avarice. He sensed Mexico was a great empire from hints drifting from time to time to the island. His levity and idle merriment evaporated, replaced by intense concentration on his Big Vision. He applied all the money he possessed to outfit the armament. He mortgaged everything, borrowed against the success of the expedition, and then used the credit of his friends.

He purchased vessels, provisions, and military stores. He invited recruits by offers of financial assistance and a liberal share of the anticipated profits. Some converted their own estates into money to equip themselves. The town of St. Jago was all a bustle. He procured six ships, some of large size, and 300 recruits enrolled in a matter of a few days. How much the governor contributed is unclear, although according to Cortes' friends, it was very little although that may not have been entirely accurate.

The objectives of the expedition according to the governor's direction were: to find men reputedly held captive in Yucatan, more importantly, to barter with the natives, and most importantly to religiously convert the natives. Cortes was directed to treat the natives with kindness and humanity. He was "to give in their allegiance to him, [the Royal Master], and to manifest it by regaling him with such comfortable presents of gold, pearls, and precious stones as, by showing their own goodwill, would secure his favor and protection."

He was to acquaint himself with the natural products of the country, with the character of the races, their institutions and progress of their civilization; and he was to send home detailed accounts of all these together with such articles as he should obtain in his intercourse with them. Finally, he was to take the utmost care to omit nothing from his survey of the country that might occur as a result to the church or his sovereign. The governor had not received authority to colonize the New World (i.e. Mexico), only to barter with the natives.

> An extreme leader has a clear Vision and develops a Plan for achieving that vision.

The Governor had Second Thoughts about Cortes' Commission

The importance given to Cortes, and perhaps his more lofty bearing, gradually made the naturally suspicious Velasquez uneasy. He became apprehensive that his officer, when away where he would have the power, might also have the inclination to throw off his dependence on the governor altogether. An incident at this time heightened these suspicions.

A half mad fellow, the governor's jester, cried out while Velasquez walked with Cortes toward the port, "Have a care, master, or we shall have to go a hunting, some day or another, after this same captain of ours!" Cortes told the governor to not heed him. "He is a saucy knave, and deserves a good whipping." However, the words had already sunk deep into Velasquez' mind. Some of the governor's kinsmen fanned the latent embers into a blaze of jealousy. They reminded Velasquez of his past quarrel with Cortes.

By misconstruing Cortes' recent actions, they convinced the governor to entrust the expedition to other hands. The governor communicated his design to his confidential advisors, Lares and Duero, who reported it without delay to Cortes. They advised him to expedite matters and to lose no time in getting his fleet to sea, if he was to retain command of it. Cortes showed his usual prompt decisiveness on this occasion, a trait that would often give direction to his destiny.

He had not assembled his full complement of men, vessels and the needed supplies. But he resolved to weigh anchor that very night. He informed his officers of his purpose and probably the cause of it. He visited a butcher and relieved him of all of his stock, leaving in payment a massive gold chain of much value that he had been wearing around his neck. At midnight when the town was asleep, the men all went quietly onboard and the little squadron dropped down the bay.

The next morning the entire town was amazed. When the news reached the governor, he sprang from his bed, dressed hastily, mounted his horse and, followed by his retinue, galloped to the port. Cortes, seeing their approach, entered an armed boat and pulled to within speaking distance of the shore.

The governor said, "And it is thus you part from me! A courteous way of taking leave, truly." Cortes responded, "Time presses, and there are some things that should be done before they are even thought of. Has your Excellency any commands?"

The mortified governor had nothing to say in return so Cortes, politely waving his hand, returned to his vessel and, on November 18, 1518, the little fleet made sail for the port of Macaca, about 15 miles distant. The governor returned to his house with the knowledge that he blundered in appointing Cortes and now probably had made him his enemy. The clandestine departure would be later severely criticized. Cortes, duly authorized by the authorities of Hispaniola, was equally at risk for his reputation and his fortune.

Cortes felt obligated to his employer in the conduct of the enterprise. From Macaca, where Cortes laid in some of his missing stores from the royal farms as an unofficial "loan from the king," he proceeded to Trinidad, a larger town on the southernmost coast of Cuba. Here he landed, erected his standard in front of his quarters and announced his mission, making liberal offers to all who would join the expedition. Volunteers came in daily including over 100 of Grijalva's men who had just returned from his voyage who wanted to return again to Mexico.

Cortes' fame attracted cavaliers of family and distinction, Hidalgos, including Pedro de Alvarado and his brothers, Cristoval de Oild, Alonso de Avila, Juan Velasquez de Leon, a near relative of the governor, Alonso Hernandez de Puertecarrero, and Gonzalo de Sandoval – all who would take important parts in the conquest. When they turned out, they were welcomed with lively strains of music and joyous salvos of artillery. Cortes acquired the military stores he felt he needed.

Learning that a trading vessel laden with grain and other commodities for the mines was off the coast, he ordered one of his caravels out to seize her and bring her into the port. He paid the master in bills for both cargo and ship and even persuaded him, a man named Seldeno, who was wealthy, to join his fortunes on the expedition. He then dispatched Diego de Ordaz to seize another ship in like manner and to meet him off Cape St. Antonio, the westerly point of the island.

He did so to temporarily distance Ortaz from his planning because he was one of the governor's household and an inconvenient spy on Cortes' actions. While Cortes was so occupied, the commander of Trinidad received letters from Velasquez ordering him to seize Cortes and detain him. The commander conveyed this information to Cortes' principal officers who counseled him to not make the attempt as it could result in a commotion among the soldiers that might end up leaving the town in ashes. He ended up ignoring the letters.

Cortes then ordered Alvarado with a small body of men to march cross-country to Havana, while he himself would sail around the westernmost point of the island and meet him there with the squadron. When he arrived, he took time to better prepare his ships and men, equipping them with thickly quilted jackets (like body armor). He organized the men into 11 companies, each under the command of an experienced officer. Some officers were friends or kin of Valesquez – he treated them equally.

His principal standard was black velvet embroidered with gold and emblazoned with a red cross amidst flames of blue and white with the motto in Latin beneath; "Friends, let us follow the cross; and under this sign, if we have faith, we shall conquer." He increased the number of domestics and officers in his household, placing himself on the footing with a man of high station – a state he would continue throughout his life. Now at age 33 or 34, he was of middle size, pale complexion, and large dark eyes, giving him a grave expression unlike his cheerful temperament.

He was slender with a deep chest, broad shoulders, muscular frame, and well proportioned. He had the combination of vigor and agility, which qualified him in fencing, horsemanship, and other chivalrous exercises. In his diet, he was temperate, careful of what he ate and drinking little; while to toil and privation he was perfectly indifferent. His dress was neither gaudy nor striking, but rich. His manners, frank and soldier-like, concealed a most cool and calculating spirit.

With his gayest humor there mingled a settled air of resolution, which made those who approached him feel they must obey; and which infused something like awe into the attachment of his most devoted followers. Such a combination, in which love was tempered by authority, was calculated to inspire devotion in the rough and turbulent spirits among whom his lot was to be cast. His character had changed with his change in circumstances – calling forth qualities from his bosom.

> Extreme leaders maintain an air of resolution. They make prompt decisions at critical moments. Extreme leaders also do not allow obstacles to impede their progress and, if necessary, will even change their character to adjust to changes in circumstances.

Cortes Sneaks out of Town

Before Cortes' preparations were completed, the commander of Havana, Don Pedro Barba, received dispatches from Velasquez ordering him to apprehend Cortes and to prevent the departure of his vessels. Cortes also received a letter requesting him to postpone his voyage until the governor could communicate with him in person. The Captain-General had the good will of Barba but even if he had not, Barba did not have the power to restrain Cortes, whose officers and men were already prepared to lay down their life for him.

Cortes wrote to Velasquez imploring him to rely on Cortes' devotion to the governor's interests and concluded with the comfortable assurance that he and the whole fleet, God willing, would sail on the following morning. On Feb. 10, 1519 the little squadron got under way and met the others at Cape St. Antonio - totaling 11 ships: one 100 tons burden, three 70 to 80 tons, and the remainder caravels and open brigantines.

The whole fleet was put under the chief pilot, Antonio de Alaminos, a veteran navigator who had served Columbus, Cordova and Grijalva in his former expedition to the Yucatan. Landing on the cape and mustering his forces, Cortes found they amounted to 110 mariners, 553 soldiers, including 32 crossbowmen and 13 Arquebusiers, and 200 Indians from the island, plus a few Indian women for menial chores. He was provisioned with 10 heavy guns, 4 lighter guns, called falconets, and a good supply of ammunition. This may sound like a formidable force but the populations of natives that Cortes would face would number in the hundreds of thousands.

He also had 16 horses, which were hard to transport in the small ships. But Cortes had rightfully estimated the importance of cavalry for their service in the field and for striking terror in the savages. He entered on a conquest with a stout heart but with a force he would have considered paltry had he foreseen half of the difficulties. Cortes addressed his men in a short but animated speech – telling them they were entering upon a noble enterprise, one that would make their names famous for ages. He was leading them to countries that only a handful of Spaniards had ever seen.

"I hold out to you a glorious prize, but it is to be won by incessant toil. Great things are achieved only by great exertions, and glory was never the reward of sloth. If I have labored hard and staked my all on this undertaking, it is for the love of that renown, which is the noblest recompense of man. But, if any among you covets riches more, be but true to me, as I will be true to you and to the occasion, and I will make you masters of such as our countrymen have never dreamed of! You are few in number, but strong in resolution; and, if this does not falter, doubt not but that the Almighty, who has never deserted the Spaniard in his conquest of the Infidel, will shield you, though encompassed by a cloud of enemies; for your cause is a just cause, and you are to fight under the banner of the Cross. Go forward then, with alacrity and confidence and carry to a glorious issue the work so auspiciously begun."

His appeal touched on the various chords of ambition, avarice and religious zeal, sent a thrill through the bosoms of his martial audience and, receiving it with acclaim, eagerly pressed forward under a chief who was to lead them not so much to battle as to what he considered triumph.

He found his own enthusiasm was largely shared by his followers. Mass was celebrated and the fleet placed under the protection of St. Peter the patron saint of Cortes. They weighed anchor and departed on Feb. 18, 1519.

The ships became separated in a storm and Cortes arrived at the island of Cozumel last. When he arrived, he found that Pedro de Alvarado, in the short time he had been there, had entered the temples, rifled them of their few ornaments, and by violent conduct terrified the natives such that they had fled into the interior of the island. Cortes was incensed, as Alvarado's actions were contrary to the policy Cortes had laid out, and he could not refrain from reprimanding his officer in the presence of the army. He commanded two Indian natives, taken by Alvadaro, be brought before him.

Through the help of an interpreter, Melchorejo, who Grijalva had brought to Cuba, he explained to them that his visit was in peace. He gave presents to them and an invitation to their countrymen for them to return to their homes without fear. Soon, the natives returned and trade began, consisting of trinkets and cutlery for gold ornaments – each party thinking that they had outwitted the other. While he sent Diego de Ordaz with two brigantines to seek on the Yucatan coast some previously captured Christians, he investigated the interior. He found a more advanced civilization than he expected.

> The essence of Cortes and of other extreme leaders is: "Great things are achieved only by great exertions, and glory was never the reward of sloth." He inspired his men by convincing them they were entering into a noble enterprise blended with, as the author wrote, " … the various chords of ambition, avarice and religious zeal."

Cortes Lands in Mexico

In 1519, Cortes landing on the coast of Mexico and proceeded to establish a colony and press his exploration toward what is today called Mexico City. During the establishment of the colony, a story arose, as it is now commonly told, that he burned his ships as a means of focusing his men on the mission ahead and by so doing put away the thoughts some held of returning to Cuba. He had recently hung two men and mutilated another who had been conspiring to sneak off with one of the ships; curiously one of those hung was the guard who had grabbed him outside that church. That should have been sufficient to deter his men from mutiny, but if he had no reason to worry about the ships, his mind would be more at ease. The truth of the matter is: He did in fact burn all but one small ship but, prior to burning them removed to storage onshore their cordage, sails, iron and all else that was movable. He burned the ships, not so much as a way to focus his men, although that was one consequence of doing so, but rather because the ships had been grievously racked by heavy gales and were worm-eaten in their sides and bottoms so as to be unseaworthy. Some were already struggling to keep afloat. The intense infestation of worms into the wood of ships was a common plague in those days that limited the life of all ships (Prescott, 1843, p. Vol. 1, 254-255). He would later build new ships when it came time for him to return to Cuba.

There is much more to Cortes' story, but we will end here because we have made our points about Cortes' leadership style. Cortes was not too scrupulous but was effective in the execution of his plans; his fame darkened by the commission of more than one act, which even his boldest apologists would find hard to vindicate. (Prescott, 1843, p. Vol. 2, 372-373)

> However, as an extreme leader, Cortes fashioned Big Visions for those he served -- his church and crown, swept away all obstacles that lay in his track, made fast, bold decisions when fast, bold decisions were needed, planned thoroughly when given the time, and accomplished his goals with alacrity.

REFERENCES

Cohen, W. A. (1990). *The Art of the Leader*. New York, NY: Prentice Hall Trade.

Fehrenbacher, D. E. (1992). Selected Speeches and Writings/Lincoln. Retrieved from http://showcase.netins.net/web/creative/lincoln/education/failures.htm

Gandhi, M. K. (1957). *The Story of My Experiments with Truth*. Boston, MA: Beacon Press.

How to Win Friends and Influence People. (1936). Retrieved from http://www.westegg.com/unmaintained/carnegie/win-friends.html

Indian Child, MAHATMA GANDHI Biography, information, Pictures. (n.d). http://www.indianchild.com/mahatma_gandhi.htm

Irving, W. (1829). *A History of the Life and Voyages of Christopher Columbus*. Paris, France: Jules Didot, Sr. and A. and W. Galignani.

Kane, D. K. (1856). *Arctic Explorations in the Years 1853, '54, '55*. Philadelphia, PA: Childs & Peterson.

Northwest Passage. (n.d.). Retrieved from http://www.absoluteastronomy.com/topics/Northwest_Passage

Patton, C. D. (2005). *Colt Terry, Green Beret*. College Station, TX: Texas A&M University Press.

Patton, C. D. (2009). *Fifteen Secrets to Successful Timeshare Management*. Orlando, FL: Xlibris Corporation.

Patton, C. D. (2009). *Strategize Your Way to Success*. New York, NY USA: Xlibris Corporation.

Peale, N. V. (1996). *The Power of Positive Thinking*. New York, NY: Balantine Books.

Prescott, W. H. (1843). *History of the Conquest of Mexico* (ed.). 150 Worth St. Corner Mission Place, New York, NY: John W. Lovell Company.

Twain, M. (1899). *Personal Recollections of Joan of Arc*. [Google Books]. Retrieved from books.google.com/books

Printed in Great Britain
by Amazon

10873097R00090